The Dagenham Girl Pipers

With very best wishes,

Linda Rhodes

Also by Linda Rhodes

THE DAGENHAM MURDER: THE BRUTAL KILLING OF PC GEORGE CLARK, 1846
by Linda Rhodes, Lee Shelden & Kathryn Abnett
(winner of the Crime Writers' Association Gold Dagger Award 2006)

"One of the most thorough books on local history one could wish to find. If your family were connected with the area or with the Metropolitan Police then this is a must for you. For the rest of us it is a very good and compelling read, and an example of how to write good local and family history". *(Cockney Ancestor Magazine)*

FOUL DEEDS & SUSPICIOUS DEATHS IN BARKING, DAGENHAM & CHADWELL HEATH
by Linda Rhodes & Kathryn Abnett

"This is an absorbing volume of chilling and dark tales which cannot fail to provoke a reaction in the reader...This book is a must for anyone interested in the history of crime". *(Local History Magazine)*

THE ROMFORD OUTRAGE: THE MURDER OF INSPECTOR THOMAS SIMMONS, 1885
by Linda Rhodes & Kathryn Abnett

"The authors have meticulously researched all the aspects of Victorian police work in connection with the murders, in great detail. A graphic and very readable case study". *(Essex Family Historian)*

THE DAGENHAM GIRL PIPERS

an 80th anniversary celebration

Linda Rhodes

Heathway Press

First published in Great Britain in 2011 by

Heathway Press
Romford, Essex

www.rhodes-research.co.uk

Enquiries about booking the Dagenham Girl Pipers, or becoming a member of the band, should be directed to:

Karen Mahoney,
the David Land Agency,
10 Wyndham Place,
London WIH 2PU.
Phone 020 7723 2456
e**mail:** karen@davidlandagency.fsnet.co.uk

CONTENTS

Detail of an early photograph of the band, 1932
(Ken & Richard Chapman collection)

Introduction
First band practice, 1930

Our story begins on the morning of Saturday 4 October 1930. Passengers on an aircraft approaching London from the east could look down upon street after street of terraced houses laid out in neat geometric patterns of straight, curved or circular roads, interspersed with cul-de-sacs (nicknamed 'banjos' by residents), and guess it was the famous Becontree Estate. Begun as a London County Council 'Homes for Heroes' project after World War One, Becontree wasn't yet finished but was well on its way to becoming the largest of its kind in the world.

It was so big that a railway had been constructed to carry building materials unloaded from the Thames at Dagenham Dock. Steam engines chugged up and down the main line, in the centre of a new road named Valence Avenue, and from time to time temporary branch lines were laid down to supply the areas under construction. To the south, amidst a forest of cranes and cables, the giant Ford factory was rapidly rising above the Thameside marshes, to be officially opened the following year, 1931.

Although the Becontree Estate also covered parts of Barking and Ilford, it lay mostly in Dagenham, which had been a thinly-populated rural Essex parish just a few years before. Looking closely, our aircraft passengers would have noticed some roads which, though lined with new houses, didn't quite fit the strict modern layout. These were the ancient highways of old Dagenham, such as Gale Street, Green Lane, Oxlow Lane and Halbutt Street.

Oxlow Lane was crossed north-south by a major new road named Heathway. South-west of that junction lay Osborne Square, with a jumble of structures to catch the eye. There was a yet-unfinished Congregational church named Osborne Hall; a canvas marquee where services were held in the meantime; and a low wooden building of typical Scout hut design.

On that October morning a dozen girls, aged around 11, made their way to the hut from various directions. On entering they spotted the familiar figures of the Reverend Joseph Waddington Graves, the Osborne Hall minister, and his wife May. With them was a tall Scotsman whose appearance in kilt, sporran and tweed jacket caused some of the youngsters to giggle.

Mr Graves must surely have been experiencing a few doubts about the extraordinary venture he was about to set in motion. He had been forced to borrow from his own insurance policies to set it up, and knew that it would take many months, if not years, of hard work before it could bear fruit. The Highlander – Pipe-Major G. Douglas Taylor, formerly of the King's Own Scottish Borderers – had scoffed at the idea at first. A girls' pipe band? Whoever heard of such a thing? And Sassenach girls at that! Would he ever be able to hold his head up again?

Yet, against all the odds, that first practice session of the Dagenham Girl Pipers led to great things. The band would rise to become a household name, performing for heads of state and royalty around the world, and is still going strong 80 years later.

Chapter 1
The founder:
Joseph Waddington Graves

At the time the band was created, Mr Graves was 49 years old. Born on 15 January 1881 above his father's chemist's shop at 158 High Street in Deal, Kent, he was named Joseph Waddington Graves after his father and grandfather. His mother, Annetta Cardew Craske, was the daughter of a Colchester auctioneer. The couple had married in 1873 and had lived in Stansted Mountfitchet and Brightlingsea, both in Essex, before moving to Deal around 1880 with their daughters Mary, Elizabeth and Minnie Annetta (known as Minna).

Just six weeks after young Joseph's birth, tragedy struck with the death of his four year-old sister Elizabeth from croup. Two more daughters, Dorothy and Brenda, were born at Deal before the family moved to nearby Sandwich. The youngest child, Robert, arrived in 1890. A few years later the family moved north to York, the native city of Joseph's father.

Young Joseph seemed to be destined to pursue his father's trade of chemist and druggist. The 1901 census describes him, aged 20, as a 'clerk in a drug store' at Burley Village in Headingley, Leeds. He also followed in his father's footsteps where religion was concerned. In his spare time, Joseph Graves senior was a Wesleyan Methodist Local Preacher. Many years later, in 1957, the younger Joseph wrote in his essay *Sixty Years a Preacher* that:

...on frequent Sundays his father puts on his best black suit, and sets off, usually on foot, to some distant village. Sometimes the boy, as he became old enough, would accompany his father on the long country walk. There his supreme delight and pride would be to watch his father ascend the pulpit of a tiny chapel...sitting in the corner of an old-fashioned pew, the boy's thoughts would not be centred on the sermon so much as wondering if he can hope to enjoy the high honour of entering a pulpit when he is old enough.

The opportunity came in June 1897, the month of Queen Victoria's Diamond Jubilee. In a small Mission Hall in York Joseph, aged 16, conducted his first full preaching service.

Joseph remained a chemist's assistant for another nine years before making a momentous decision in 1906. At that time, the newly-founded Canadian frontier province of Saskatchewan was appealing for migrants. They should expect hard work in harsh conditions, but the opportunities and rewards could also be great. Joseph, then 25 and unmarried, decided to try his luck across the Atlantic. On 15 March 1906 he left Liverpool on the *Parisian,* travelling in steerage (the lowest class of accommodation). His family remained in England.

On arrival in Canada, Joseph took whatever work was available, with the ultimate aim of saving enough money to enter theological college to train as a minister. His jobs included spells as a store detective, bronco buster and even a medium for a professional hypnotist! His religious faith was still paramount, however, and he later fondly recalled being a Sky Pilot (slang term for a missionary) on the prairies of Saskatchewan. Eventually Joseph was able to begin his studies – first at Winnipeg, Manitoba, then at the Wesleyan Theological College in Montreal, part of McGill University.

In 1909, after three years in Canada, Joseph sailed back to see his parents, who were now living in Leeds. After a three-month visit he departed from Liverpool on the *Lusitania*. He would never see his mother Annetta again. She died in 1910 aged 64, and his father followed three years later aged 66.

World War One broke out in August 1914. After Mr Graves completed his degree in 1915 he was appointed a Padre with the Canadian Army. He accompanied the troops to the Western Front, where he was twice buried in the trenches and suffered permanent shrapnel scars. At the end of the war in 1918 Mr Graves sailed back to Canada, but not to resume his peacetime life. Instead, he had signed up for the 4000-strong Canadian Expeditionary Force to Siberia. The Russian Civil War was then raging in the wake of the 1917 Revolution, and the Expeditionary Force aimed to help the White Russians oust Lenin's Communist government. It did not succeed, however, and the Canadians were recalled without a battle being fought.

CAPTAIN JOSEPH WADDINGTON GRAVES, B. D.

Mr Graves sailed from Yokohama, Japan, back to Canada in July 1919. This episode had lasted only a matter of months, but had a huge impact on his life. While with the Expeditionary Force he had come across a three-year-old Armenian orphan girl living in wretched conditions. Her plight so affected him that he adopted her, calling her Brenda, the name of both his youngest sister and of an aunt who had lived with the family during his childhood.

Mr Graves in Canadian military uniform, from his book *The Renaissance of Korea*

Mr Graves's next step was to take further studies in Divinity at Yale University in Connecticut, USA. Crossing the border from Canada to the USA en route to Yale in September 1919 he was recorded as 38 years old, 5 feet 6 inches tall, with brown hair and blue eyes.

During his time in Siberia and the Far East Mr Graves had also visited Korea, then under Japanese occupation. In March 1919 a protest march in Seoul against the imposition of Japanese culture on their own traditional way of life ended tragically when Japanese troops opened fire. Mr Graves's interest in Korean history and culture, together with his sense of outrage at what was happening, led him to write a book, *The Renaissance of Korea,* which was published in Yale in 1920.

After one academic year at Yale, Mr Graves prepared to return to England. He applied for, and obtained, the post of sub-warden at Browning Hall, which was attached to the York Street Chapel in Walworth, South London. Named after the poet Robert Browning, who had been baptized at the chapel in 1812, it was a Christian community centre supporting causes such as adult education and trade unionism. Back in 1908 it had been the venue of a conference which led to the introduction of Old Age Pensions in Britain.

Joseph Graves had not long been at Browning Hall when its founder, the Reverend Francis Herbert Stead, retired, leaving him in sole charge. Another milestone in his life occurred on 1 May 1924 when, at the age of 43, he married 21 year-old schoolteacher May Stroud. The wedding took place at York Street Chapel, and the bride was the daughter of James Stroud, a bookbinder's foreman from Larcom Street, off Southwark Road. Joseph and May had a ready-made family with his adopted daughter, Brenda, but were to have no children of their own.

Mr Graves meeting the Duke and Duchess of York (later King George VI and Queen Elizabeth) in the 1920s while warden of Browning Hall *(Bette Read)*

Mr Graves spent ten years at Browning Hall before his momentous appointment as the first Congregationalist Minister at Osborne Hall. He presided over his first service in Dagenham on the evening of Easter Sunday, 20 April 1930. As we have seen, the newly-built Becontree Estate was huge, and there was an obvious need for places of worship to keep pace with the increase in population. Despite having to use a marquee while his church was being built, Mr Graves had an enthusiastic congregation and a thriving Sunday school.

Mr Graves recognized that the people of Becontree could not form a distinct community without some shared traditions. So with typical boldness, one of his first acts was to bring the ancient ceremony of the May Queen into the modern housing estate. His Sunday school pupils voted for the May Queen amongst themselves, and their choice fell on 11 year-old Edith Turnbull.

On the early morning of Thursday 1 May, Edith was brought from her home in Alibon Road to Osborne Square, in a decorated cart, attended by heralds, ladies-in-waiting, and maids of honour. A crown of wild pansies surmounted her long ringlets of auburn hair, and her attendants wore white gowns & garlands of primroses.

The building of Osborne Hall had to be financed by a large loan. Donations towards its cost were pouring in – *the Times* reported on 18 December 1930 that two anonymous gifts of £1,200 had been received. Yet there was still a large shortfall. Mr Graves pondered fundraising opportunities, and it was at this point that the idea of a pipe band entered his head. He later wrote that 'During all of my life that I can recall, bagpipes have fascinated me'. The pipes had always been played by men, and Mr Graves never revealed when and why he decided to create a girls' band. When pressed, he would shrug his shoulders and say 'There isn't an explanation. It just happened!'

Much preparation needed to be done, of course. An instructor had to be employed, and instruments and uniforms purchased. As we have seen, Mr Graves was forced to borrow from his insurance policies to finance the project. The teacher he chose, Pipe-Major G. Douglas Taylor, lived in London and had recently published a book of traditional Scottish dances. He had served for many years with the King's Own Scottish Borderers, and had been awarded the Distinguished Conduct Medal for his actions during the Battle of Loos in 1915. At first, Mr Taylor just laughed at the idea of a girls' pipe band, but he was eventually won over. Alfred Haynes, in his 1957 book *the Dagenham Girl Pipers*, quotes him as saying 'I hae me doots, but when do we start?'

Mr Graves chose twelve girls from his Sunday school to form the band, beginning with the May Queen, Edith Turnbull. He displayed confidence about the future success of the band from the outset. On seeking permission from the parents of 11 year-old Peggy Iris, he said that by joining the band the girls would take part in the Lord Mayor's Show, and one day march along Broadway in New York. They must have found this impossible to believe - but he would eventually be proved right!

Chapter 2
The 1930s

Pipe Major Taylor began by numbering the girls according to the alphabetical order of their surnames. Margaret Battley was number 1, Violet Clark 2, Gladys Cooper 3, Gladys Cross 4, Peggy Iris 5, Violet Johnson 6, Joyce Jones 7, Edna Jordan 8, Violet Nash 9, Doris Patterson 10, Phyllis Seabrook 11 and Edith Turnbull at number 12.

Ahead of them lay the lengthy task of mastering this complex and challenging musical instrument. After that first session in October 1930, much of their time outside school was devoted to practice. They met Saturday mornings at the hall in Osborne Square plus several evenings during the week, including regular Wednesdays in the sitting-room of nearby 27 Northfield Road, the terraced LCC house in which Mr and Mrs Graves were living until the Manse in Osborne Square was ready for them. The girls also had to learn practice exercises at home between sessions.

It would be a long time before they could handle actual bagpipes. They began by learning the fingering on practice chanters, recorder-like instruments which produced relatively quiet, low-pitched notes. Scales were followed by simple tunes, and basic notes were embellished by the addition of the ornamental grace notes which play an important role in bagpipe music.

Mr Graves's aim was a group in the military marching band tradition: pipes, drums, marching and counter-marching. At this stage in the band's development, new girls were taken on just to learn drumming, so the practice

Osborne Square in the early days, the sports hut to the right of the marquee *(Tony Clifford)*

hall was soon resounding to the sounds of the side-drums (also known as snare drums), the larger tenor drums and the bass drum (or big drum). Classes in Highland dancing followed, the repertoire including Reels, Strathspeys, the Highland Fling and the Sword Dance (danced over traditional Scottish claymores, or double-handed broadswords). The girls had no actual uniform yet, but wore practice dresses stitched by Mrs Graves.

By the summer of 1931 the band was making great progress. Mr and Mrs Graves had a thatched holiday cottage named 'Restawhyle' at Great Sampford, in rural north-west Essex, and invited Mr Taylor and the girls to spend two weeks there. During this stay the girls took delivery of their first set of bagpipes: half the regular size, but otherwise identical to standard ones, consisting of a sheepskin bag, mouthpiece, chanter for fingering and three tall pipes called 'drones'. Mr Taylor taught the girls how to look after the pipes, how to pack them, and even how to lubricate the inside of the bag with treacle to make it airtight and pliable.

The cottage was in an isolated position about two miles outside Great Sampford itself, so no neighbours could complain about the noise of the girls' first attempts. They were soon playing and marching in unison. Although pipe bands are under the control of the Pipe Major, their marching is led by a Drum Major, swinging a mace (or staff) to keep time and communicate signals to the others, such as the approaching changing or ending of a tune. The signal to finish from the Drum Major is followed by a double beat from the bass drummer, so the band has two signals to follow. Gladys Cooper assumed the Drum Major role, striding confidently ahead of the girls as they marched up and down the lane outside the cottage.

Mr Graves chose a motto for the band, the Latin phrase 'Auctor Pretiosa Facit'. Taken from a work by the Roman poet Ovid, it translates as 'The giver adds value to the gift'. A badge or logo was also designed, incorporating the Latin motto, a laurel wreath, thistles, the initials of Mr Graves (JWG) and Mr Taylor (GDT), and the date 1930.

Eighteen months after that first practice session, Pipe-Major Taylor judged that the girls were ready to perform in public. Mr Graves now had to delve further into his savings to equip them with proper Highland uniforms. The question of which tartan they should adopt was soon answered. As we have seen, Mr Taylor had belonged to the King's Own Scottish Borderers, which wore the Royal Stewart (or Stuart) tartan, the personal tartan of the Royal Family. It would obviously be best for the girls' uniforms to match his, so Royal Stewart was chosen.

The pipers' uniforms consisted of woollen kilts, fringed plaids fastened at the shoulder by a large circular silver brooch set with amber, and a sporran made from black and white horse hair. Their black velvet jackets had silver buttons, and lace adorned their collars and cuffs. They wore brogues with buckles for normal occasions and thin-soled laced shoes for dancing, and their tartan socks (or hose) sported red flashes. Pipers wore black velvet Balmoral bonnets adorned with a cock feather and another large silver brooch. Drum Majors, on the other hand, wore a Glengarry hat, plus white leather gauntlets for easier handling of the mace.

Early photographs show the drummers wearing long-sleeved tartan dresses, made by Mrs Graves. Later they would wear the full piper uniform surmounted by heavy leopard skins for bass drummers, and pale leather for tenor drummers.

The first show of the Dagenham Girl Pipers was given to an audience of their parents on 1 April 1932. So far, the band's existence had not been publicized, but Mr Taylor and Mr Graves were now confident that the time was right to tell the world. Invitations were sent to newspapers and press agencies to attend the band's first public concert, on an outdoor stage behind Osborne Hall on Friday 20 May.

The band on the stage outside Osborne Hall in 1932. Note the drummers are wearing dresses, not kilts *(Ken & Richard Chapman collection)*

The band's line-up had changed somewhat since it was originally formed. Some girls had left, for various reasons, and their replacements included Mr Graves's own daughter Brenda. According to the *Dagenham Post*, the pipers at the first public concert were: Margaret Battley, Gladys Cooper, Gladys Cross, Brenda Graves, Peggy Iris, Edna Jordan, Violet Nash, Doris Patterson, Phyllis Seabrook, Maisie Thomson and Edith Turnbull, plus reserves Jennie Baillie, Margaret Bain and Kitty McLeod.

For all who had the privilege to be there, it must have been an unforgettable and magical afternoon. Each number was received with growing enthusiasm. Even hard-bitten pressmen were captivated.

The *Star* reporter wrote 'With a brave swagger, heads thrown back and kilts swinging, they strode past me to the strains of an old Scottish battle-song...Their spirited playing was thrilling to hear'. The *Ilford Recorder* declared 'For nearly two hours the reporters were treated to a programme of marches, reels, Strathspeys, laments and sword dances, all of which were played and executed with considerable skill by the youthful pipers and dancers'.

The *Dagenham Post* told its readers that 'Clad in full Highland costume the girls made a picturesque sight, and although they tackled several difficult pieces they acquitted themselves well...They want to demonstrate that Dagenham can produce girl pipers as well as Ford cars'. The paper also mentioned that a 'considerable sum of money' had been needed for the venture. 'Although Mr Graves is in no means affluent circumstances, he has found every penny of this himself". It stated that once £500 had been raised to clear the new buildings at Osborne Hall of debt, the band would fund-raise for approved charities.

Over a hundred newspapers picked up the story, and cinemagoers up and down the country watched two minutes of highlights of the performance on the Pathé newsreel, beginning with 'NOT BRAEMAR- DAGENHAM!!! Not one is Scotch - not one has ever seen Scotland! The only Girl Pipers' Band, perfect after 18 months secret training - make first appearance'. Messrs Graves and Taylor were predictably bombarded with requests for bookings, but turned them all down. Instead, they made the girls practice even harder and extend their repertoire of tunes.

Three months later, with the school summer holidays just around the corner, Mr Graves was finalizing plans for the band's first performances outside Dagenham. The place he chose was somewhere

Marching through Dagenham in the early 1930s
(*Ken & Richard Chapman collection*)

very close to his heart – the area where he had been born and brought up. On 30 July the girls, in full uniform, took the ferry from Tilbury to Gravesend and made their way to Worth Court in Sandwich, home of William Rose, who was Mayor of Sandwich and an old friend of Mr Graves. During their ten-day stay the girls camped in tents in the grounds.

They paraded into the centre of Sandwich, and were excited but a little nervous to hear the town crier announce their first concert there, to take place in the market place. After the concert, Mr Graves preached in the town's

Baptist chapel. When the band paraded through Deal on Bank Holiday Monday (which was at that time the first Monday in August) the crowds gave them a rousing reception, and there was a poignant moment when they halted outside the shop in the High Street over which Mr Graves had been born 51 years before.

As summer turned to autumn, the girls were thrilled to hear that one of Mr Graves's seemingly impossible predictions would soon come true – they were invited to take part in the Lord Mayor's Show! On the day itself they took their place, flanked by Mr Graves and Pipe Major Taylor, and began the long march from Mansion House through the City of London. In his 1957 book *The Dagenham Girl Pipers*, Alfred H. Haynes described the reaction of the crowds lining the route:

> As, led by their 13 year-old Drum Major wielding her mace with all the adroitness and aplomb of a seasoned veteran, the small figures of the Dagenham Girl Pipers marched into view, the crowd literally gasped with amazement. So deafening was the thunderous applause which followed that the *Daily Mail* was moved to say of the girls next day: 'They were the best thing in the whole Show'.

At that time, the school-leaving age was the end of the term in which a youngster reached their 14th birthday. By the beginning of January 1933, two of the pipers had reached that age. This was the era of the Great Depression, and most girls from the Becontree Estate would be expected to contribute to their family's income by taking factory jobs, often working 45 hours a week, including Saturday mornings.

Mr Graves knew that if this happened, the band would suffer just when it was gaining renown. The only solution was to make it a full-time organization, with the pipers as paid employees and himself as manager. It would benefit the girls themselves too, as he later explained. 'The girls, who would otherwise leave school for poorly-paid employment with little or no prospects, are paid a proper wage and are given at the same time an opportunity of seeing the world, of meeting all kinds of people, and of obtaining a certain amount of culture'.

So the older girls now worked full-time for the band. Over the coming months, the others were added to the payroll. New recruits were also taken on, with one proviso: they had to be resident in Dagenham. Girls generally joined the band at 11 or 12, while still schoolgirls, and passed into the full-time ranks at 14. By 1937, the weekly wage for a 14 year-old was 9s 8d, plus 4d National Insurance. After a year she received an increment of 2s 6d.

Evening and Saturday morning practice sessions always began with prayers and a Thought for the Day. There followed half an hour of PT (physical training), the younger girls being instructed by Brenda Graves. It was essential for them to gain fitness and stamina, as they might have to go on long, tiring journeys before having to march for miles while playing or drumming, followed by a dancing display!

The girls then split into small groups for half-hour sessions, which rotated between dancing, marching, drumming and piping, before coming together for a final session. Beginners, of course, would concentrate on their chanter practice. Everyone would gather round the noticeboard to read the monthly Company Orders. Here they would learn about upcoming bookings and which girls would take part in them. In the early days the girls' names were not given in the Orders, just their individual band numbers. The number of girls needed for each show varied according to the type of engagement, ranging from full marching bands to just a piper and a dancer for a cabaret show or a Burns

Night supper. The girls didn't remain in the same groupings, but were shuffled around so that they mixed with different people from show to show. The most junior girls might be called upon just to sell postcards of the band at an event, rather than actually taking part! Supplemental Orders were issued giving details of each individual engagement.

The girls were subject to strict rules, including no make-up, no smoking and no drinking. They were chaperoned by Mrs Graves or other women, and on tours were forbidden to leave their hotels unaccompanied.

Soon after the 1932 Lord Mayor's Show the band had begun their recording career, making two discs of traditional Scottish tunes at Decca Studios. On 14 January 1933 they appeared at the Royal Albert Hall for the first time. Even after three encores, the audience still demanded more. Their programme now included recitals of humorous poems in Scottish dialect by Jennie Baillie, who was from a Scottish family.

April 1933 saw the band on their first overseas trip. A band of 25 spent five days in Belgium as part of a 'Peace Pilgrimage' of exchange visits between English and Belgian teenagers. There was concern when Violet Nash was admitted to Oldchurch Hospital with pneumonia just before the trip, but fortunately she made a full recovery. On arriving in Belgium the band settled into their base at Bruges.

On 21 April they visited Ypres, scene of much heavy fighting during World War One, which had ended less than 15 years before. After a reception at the Town Hall, they marched with a local band named Ypriania to the Menin Gate memorial to soldiers who have no known grave. The *Last Post* and *Reveille* were sounded underneath the Gate, the Pipers played a lament, then an English and a Belgian girl together laid a wreath of roses with the inscription 'Pax', meaning 'Peace'. The ceremony was broadcast live on the radio. The

Scenes from the band's 1933 visit to Belgium (*Ken & Richard Chapman collection*)

band also visited Tyne Cot Cemetery, with its Memorial to the Missing. Mr Graves admitted his own wartime memories came surging back at this time.

During this trip the girls also played at the opening of the Ghent flower festival, attended by the King and Queen of the Belgians. On 23 April they performed at a St George's Day ceremony at Zeebrugge.

On their return to Dagenham, a Welcome Home concert was held, at which the band received a thunderous reception. Tickets were 3d each, with all proceeds donated to the distress fund for strikers involved in a dispute at Briggs Bodies, which manufactured car bodies for Fords.

The band's success was now causing problems for Mr Graves, as he strove to combine it with his work as a Church Minister. Managing the band was taking up more and more of his time, of course, but there was another difficulty. Many people at the time didn't believe that entertainment could be a 'respectable' career for young women. For some, as Peggy Iris later recalled, the idea was 'downright wicked!' Ironically, the wholesome image of the Dagenham Girl Pipers themselves would later help put paid to this attitude.

Back in November 1932 Mr Graves had announced his resignation from the Ministry, only to withdraw it, but this only postponed the inevitable. In July 1933 he preached his final sermon at Osborne Hall.

During the summer of 1933 the band appeared in many processions, including Barking Carnival, where they marched with the band of the Grenadier Guards. In August they spent a week at Southend-on-Sea, based at the Congregational Church. The following month Edith Turnbull and Gladys Cross played for the Scottish Duke of Atholl at a lunch in Croydon.

In November 1933 the band marched in the Lord Mayor's Show for the second time. The previous month they had played three tunes for the Lord

The band with their first Pipe Major, G. Douglas Taylor *(Ken & Richard Chapman collection)*

Mayor at his official residence, Mansion House. In January 1934 they returned to the City of London to give a one-hour show at the Guildhall.

The resignation of Mr Graves from Osborne Hall meant that the band had to find new headquarters, and early in 1934 they were welcomed to St George's Church Hall in Rogers Road by its vicar the Reverend H.S.J. Marshall. Around the same time, the band lost the services of Pipe Major Taylor, who had been unable to commit himself to them full-time as he also ran a piping academy in London. Pipe Major Charles Cameron, of the Queen's Own Cameron Highlanders, was appointed in his place, to be joined in July 1934 by his brother Allan Cameron.

A system of promotions within the band was now introduced, similar to that in the British Army. Gladys Cross, Edith Turnbull and Gladys Cooper were all appointed Corporals, and had a stripe sewn onto the right sleeve of their jackets. The band was now 50 strong, so could be divided into several units performing in different places at the same time. In March 1934 they appeared again at the Royal Albert Hall, to an enthusiastic audience of 8,000.

Pipe Major Charles Cameron meeting the band in 1934 *(Ken & Richard Chapman collection)*

Nearer home, the following month the girls performed at Trinity Methodist Church, Romford. Their repertoire now included English folk tunes and well-known hymns as well as traditional Scottish tunes. To lend variety to their two-hour performances, the girls were now being trained as a choir. Their singing instructor was William Parkyn, a well-known organist and concert director of East Ham Central Hall.

A landmark in the band's history was reached in May 1934 when they began to use standard-sized pipes instead of their original half-sized ones. Lily Vale, who joined the band that year, recalls that:

> In those early years of the band being introduced to a wider audience, publicity played a big part in our recognition...We would leave our homes to assemble for an engagement, all spruced up with our uniforms on and carrying our instruments. Other children would stop and stare and follow, as we met up with our own friends from street to street, word soon got around something was happening in Dagenham. A coach would take us to our venue, but we always formed and piped our way

in...We paraded and piped the last few hundred yards, it drew attention, what publicity! And we enjoyed the sight of the crowds that gathered.

In June 1934 the band played before the Prince of Wales (later Edward VIII and Duke of Windsor) at the Northampton Agricultural Show, in Kettering. They performed *God save the Prince of Wales* in his honour. The Pipers toured various parts of Britain that summer, including the West Country and the North of England. The Northern trip saw three of the girls performing in the towns of their birth: Edith Turnbull and her sister Mary in South Shields, and Kitty McLeod in Sunderland.

Another visit was to the Isle of Man, where they appeared at a traditional Highland Gathering. Gladys Cooper was the first female Drum Major ever to take part in such an event, but proved the star of the show. She marched alongside veteran drum majors of famous Highland pipe bands, and according to the press 'gave a demonstration of staff swinging which in some ways equalled their own'. On leaving the arena she was mobbed by the crowd.

The band's engagements at home that summer included the annual parade and service of the Dagenham Old Contemptibles Association. Its members had all served with the British Expeditionary Force in 1914, when the Kaiser had called them 'A contemptible little army!' Mr Graves was the Association's chaplain, and the band performed at many events on its behalf over the years.

That summer the band took its first flight, from Heston Aerodrome to the Isle of Wight, where they took part in the Ryde Carnival. A battery of reporters and film cameramen watched as the girls played a farewell march before entering two airliners, both of which were appropriately manufactured by Ford (but not made in Dagenham!).

In October 1934 the band paraded through the streets of Barking before launching its winter season of concerts at the Methodist Central Hall in East

Street. Piper Jennie Baillie gave her popular humorous recitations, and her monologue *The best dressed Highlander* received a huge ovation from the audience of 1,200. Pipe Major Allan Cameron, an expert Highland dancer, gave two solo dances. The band were mobbed as they climbed into their coach for the journey back to Dagenham.

Mr and Mrs Graves had now moved into Raydons House (now 28-30 Raydons Road), one of the few surviving old Dagenham farmhouses. It served as the band's headquarters for many years, and they also had the use of the Methodist Central Hall in Heathway as a practice venue. More promotions were announced. Gladys Cross and Edith Turnbull became Sergeants, while Peggy Iris and Phyllis Seabrook rose to Corporal. A few months later Peggy was promoted to Sergeant and Kitty McLeod to Corporal.

Drum Major Gladys Cooper
(Ken & Richard Chapman collection)

November 1934 was a busy month for the band. After marching in the Lord Mayor's Show for the third year running, they headed straight to Chadwell Heath to perform at the Embassy Cinema in the High Road. Later renamed the Gaumont Palace, the Embassy had opened a few months earlier as a magnificent venue for both cinema and live variety shows. The band was also regularly on the bill at the equally luxurious Mayfair Cinema in Whalebone Lane, Beacontree Heath, and in July 1936 played at the grand opening of the Heathway Cinema (later renamed the Odeon).

Two views of the band's early flights, 1934 (above, *Ken & Richard Chapman collection;* below, *Dagenham Girl Pipers Veterans' Association*)

By this time the Pipers were also much in demand in the mass media. They played for radio from Broadcasting House, with Drum Major Gladys Cooper bravely speaking live on air during the interval, and the same month were filmed at the Universal Film News studio in London's Wardour Street.

The band still made regular appearances in their home town, however, such as when two girls piped in the haggis at the Dagenham Caledonian Society's

1935 Burns Night dinner at the Chequers Inn. In February the band performed at Beacontree Heath Methodist Church in aid of a gymnastics club.

The same month, they began a two-week tour of Wales. It included a visit to Gresford Pit, scene of a recent catastrophe which had killed 265 miners. The band played a sorrowful lament, which was much appreciated. A local lady councillor praised them for setting themselves to master a difficult instrument, in contrast to popular jazz bands playing what she called 'paper trumpets'.

In May 1935 the band performed at the official opening of the Elm Park housing estate and railway station, just a few miles east of Dagenham. That year King George V and Queen Mary were celebrating their Silver Jubilee. The girls competed amongst themselves in a Jubilee March Contest, in which they had to compose a two-part Quick March for bagpipes. The winning entry, from bass drummer Elsie Spooner, was published as the *Dagenham Jubilee March* and played at the band's many Jubilee Year engagements. Elsie was also invited to give a half-hour talk on BBC radio later that year.

In November 1935 the band welcomed an additional Pipe Major, Mr Thomas Kinross Marshall, born in Stirling. A momentous tour was approaching – the band's first visit to Scotland. In 1933 they had been asked to play at the Cowal Highland Gathering at Dunoon, but were forced to decline owing to other bookings.

Bass drummer Elsie Spooner
(Ken & Richard Chapman collection)

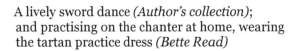
A lively sword dance *(Author's collection)*;
and practising on the chanter at home, wearing
the tartan practice dress *(Bette Read)*

The band left for Scotland on 11 November. Following a successful week in a variety show at the Empress Theatre in Glasgow, the first engagements on their tour proper attracted only small audiences. Why was this, everyone wondered? Was it bad weather, poor advertising, or were the Scots prejudiced against the idea of an English girls' pipe band?

As they travelled north, the weather worsened, but good reviews and word of mouth gave them bigger audiences and enthusiastic receptions, especially in Inverness, home city of the Cameron brothers. Mr Graves paid a brief visit, and returned to tell the press the band were now enjoying full halls. From the far north of Scotland they journeyed down the eastern coast to Edinburgh, where they appeared for a week at Waverley Market.

The tour was cut short by the death of George V on 20 January 1936. The band headed back to Dagenham, where they played a series of Laments for the

Dead in memory of the late King at the very time his funeral was taking place at Windsor. In March 1936 the band headed north once more, this time for a tour of Northern England which included a programme of marches on the Bishop of Durham's private lawn.

The band was now a regular feature at sporting events such as football league matches. Edith Turnbull had piped solo at an international between England and France at Boulogne. When the band appeared at a match in May 1936 between Leyton Orient and Motherwell, the press noted that 'More than half the tunes were a breakaway from the conventional Scottish tunes....included were a number of old wartime tunes of the *Tipperary* type, and the effect was very pleasing'.

Closer to home, that same month a Double Band (two complete bands, each led by a Drum Major) played at the RAF base at Hornchurch on Empire Day to a crowd of 13,000. They gave shows both in the open and inside a large hangar. In July 1936 an even larger group, of four complete bands, marched from Heathway along Church Elm Lane and into the Glebe Road football ground for the annual parade of the Old Contemptibles Association.

That summer there was great excitement when the band was invited to perform at the closing ceremony of the 1936 Olympic Games at Berlin

An unusual early group photograph
(Ken & Richard Chapman collection)

Postcard showing a double band: enough performers for two complete bands *(Author's collection)*

(remembered as the Nazi Olympics, and for the four gold medals won by legendary black American sprinter Jesse Owens). Two days before the Pipers were due to fly to Berlin, however, officials insisted that they needed individual passports rather than a group one. There wasn't sufficient time to obtain the documents, so sadly the band was unable to fulfil this once-in-a-lifetime engagement.

At the band's sixth birthday celebration, in October 1936, it was announced that 17 year-old Edith Turnbull had been appointed to the highest rank in the band, that of Pipe Major. She became the world's first female and first non-Scottish Pipe Major. The story made international headlines, and the front page of the *Dagenham Post* was dominated by an article headed 'From May Queen to Pipe Major'. Edith could now be distinguished from the other girls by the ornate braiding of her jacket, and by the four stripes on the right sleeve surmounted by an embroidered stylized design in the shape of a set of pipes.

Edith Turnbull as a youngster in ringlets
(above); and as Pipe Major in 1936
(*Ken & Richard Chapman collection*)

The following year she was presented with a special silk Pipe Major's banner, made by Mrs Graves and featuring the band's crest.

A humorous article in November 1936 pointed out that 'Guy Fawkes proving a great friend to the pipers. They are invited to play at an increased number of bonfire celebrations engagements, and the girls are learning to be quite unmoved in a perfect rain of squibs. But it does take considerable nerve to continue piping or dancing with loud bangs all around'.

The New Year of 1937 found the band in Belgium once more, scene of their first overseas trip back in 1933. They played in cabaret at the Hotel Atlanta in

Brussels, and one evening were thrilled to see legendary French entertainer Maurice Chevalier in the audience and meet him afterwards. The girls also travelled to the nearby battlefield of Waterloo, where they played patriotic marches including *the British Grenadiers*.

Back home, the band performed on stage during the opening week of the new Gaumont Palace Cinema at Camden Town in January. For this engagement they unveiled a new development: syncopated music on the bagpipes, united with the stage orchestra and the cinema organ. As well as the finer points of the music, much thought had to go into the placement of the members of the orchestra, so that the pipers and drummers were given space to proceed up the steps and march in formation across the stage. On other occasions the band were accompanied on the accordion or piano by one of their own number, Beatrice ('Beattie') Morrison, an accomplished musician who had trained at the Royal College of Music.

An apt caption for drummers: 'The Big Noise' *(Ken & Richard Chapman collection)*

The following month, February 1937, was an adventurous one for the band. One unit travelling along the North Wales coast in rough weather had waves sweeping over their train. Another was on its way home from Stevenage when the coach broke down, leaving the girls stranded on the road all night. Luckily Mr Graves managed to find a transport café and obtain supplies of tea and hot meat pies!

The same month saw 44 girls performing at the Gaumont British Carnival Ball at the Royal Albert Hall. Their numbers included the popular Noel Gay song *The Fleet's in port again.* The audience of over 8,000 shouted 'Dagenham! Dagenham!' as the band took their places for the finale. Two girls singled out for praise in the press were Drum Major Florrie Kenningale and bass drummer Elsie Spooner, 'with her drumstick wizardry, surely one of the most brilliant girl drummers in any band'.

That spring the band also appeared in a film *Talking Feet* with child star Hazel Ascot. The plot involved the little girl and her friends staging a charity concert to save a hospital.

In August 1937 a party of girls, led by Edith Turnbull and attended by both Mr and Mrs Graves, sailed from Dover for a German tour which was due to last a month but was extended to four due to popular demand. They appeared for a month at the Wintergarten Theatre in Berlin as part of the city's 700th

Drum Major Florrie Kenningale
(author's collection)

anniversary celebrations. Adolf Hitler, German Chancellor since 1933, attended a performance there, and told Mr Graves, through an interpreter, how impressed he was and that he wished Germany had a similar band.

As the girls marched through Berlin the following morning, they paused outside the Chancellery, and Hitler appeared on the balcony to listen to them play *It's a long way to Tipperary*. During the band's many parades along Unter den Linden, Berlin's main avenue, it was, oddly enough, British wartime

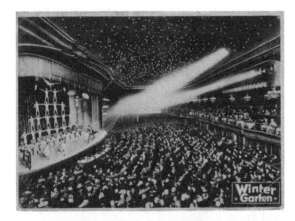

The German tour of 1937: left, the Wintergarten Theatre, Berlin *(LBBD Archives at Valence House);* below, the band in Stuttgart *(Barking & Dagenham Post)*

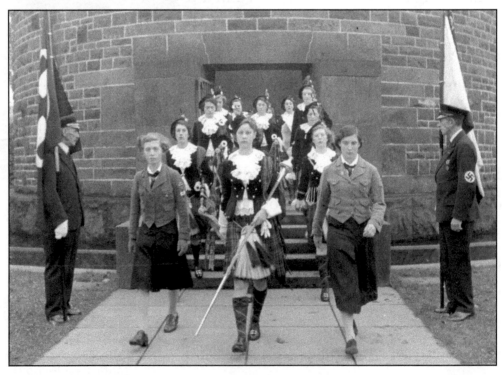

tunes such as *Tipperary* and *Keep the home fires burning* that generated the loudest cheers. After visits to Frankfurt, Bad Homburg and Stuttgart, the band spent a week in Brussels before returning to England in early December.

While the German tour was taking place, other units back in Britain played at the big Radiolympia radio and television exhibition and at various fetes and carnivals, including the Isle of Wight and Hastings. It was while she was at Hastings that 18 year-old Peggy Iris learned she had been promoted to Pipe Major. The Cameron brothers and Pipe Major George Alexander Greenfield having resigned their posts, the musical direction of the band was now the responsibility of Pipe Major Marshall, Edith Turnbull as Senior Pipe Major and Peggy as Assistant Pipe Major.

The band performed at the Gaumont Palace Cinema, Camden Town, for a week in February 1938. During the run they were joined by Will Fyffe, the popular Dundee-born character actor and variety entertainer, best known for writing and performing songs such as *Sailing up the Clyde, She was the Belle of the Ball and I belong to Glasgow*. Will Fyffe was to prove a staunch supporter of the band over the years. In 1945 he wrote: 'What I like about them is that they are like one big family, modest, unassuming, and the best-behaved lot of girls I have ever met'.

In February 1938 the band were back in their home town to play at the official opening of the New Hall building at Kingsley Hall, a Christian community centre in Parsloes Avenue. Like Osborne Hall, it had started in a marquee in 1929. It had been founded by Doris and Muriel Lester as a branch of their original Kingsley Hall in Bow. Back in 1931 Mahatma Gandhi had spent a day at the Dagenham Kingsley Hall while in London for a conference on Indian independence, during which he chose to sleep at Kingsley Hall in Bow, rather than a luxury hotel.

The following month, March 1938, a band crossed the North Sea once more to visit Holland. As they marched through the streets of Eindhoven, the crowds were so dense that the police had to use cars to clear the way before Florrie Kenningale could swing her mace. Their arrival was filmed and the newsreel shown in cinemas across Europe. When they performed at a cinema in the Hague, it was noticed that the audience included ambassadors from 14 countries.

April 1938 saw a new challenge for the girls when they performed at an ice hockey match between England and Scotland at Earls Court. As the headlines put it, 'Pipers had to tread carefully!' in special overshoes. Despite the difficulties, Peggy Iris led them in a spectacular display of piping, marching and dancing in front of an appreciative crowd of 6,000. She took the band to another unusual venue on Easter Monday later that month – Dagenham

Leading Side Drummer, Leading Piper, Drum Major & Bass Drummer
(Ken & Richard Chapman collection)

speedway track, off Ripple Road. The *Dagenham Post* noted that 'a cinder track, especially when cut up by racing cars and cycles, does not make the best foundation for marching and Highland dancing. All the same, the band gave a highly creditable performance, and received hearty applause from the big crowd'. A part band stayed on to give a cabaret show in the clubhouse later that evening.

Later that month Peggy, supported by Mrs Graves, led 16 girls on a five-month Scandinavian tour. Leaving Tilbury on the *SS Suecia,* the band stood on an upper deck where they could be seen by the crowd on the quay, and played the Highland march the *79ths Farewell to Gibraltar*. Reaching Stockholm, they were accommodated at the Astoria Hotel, which flew the Union Flag during their visit.

During the Denmark leg of the tour, the band appeared at the Tivoli Gardens Amusement Park in Copenhagen, and formed a guard of honour for King Christian at a civic function. They were brought down to earth one day, though, when an English passer-by, seeing them in full uniform in the street, asked 'What orphanage are they from?'

Meanwhile, other units were busy with stage performances back in England. A band under Doris Patterson played at many London venues with the popular Bobby Howell dance band, which had a regular radio slot at the time. In May 1938 a band led by Edith Turnbull spent a week at the New Theatre, Northampton. The Australian cricket team, captained by batsman Don Bradman, the era's biggest sporting superstar, happened to be in England on an Ashes tour. The band were asked to welcome the Australians at Northampton Station, then lead them in procession through crowded streets to the cricket ground. Don Bradman was so impressed by the band he asked them to play encores.

DAGENHAM GIRL PIPERS
"DRUM MAJOR"   Copyright
J. W. Graves, Dagenham

(Ken & Richard Chapman collection)

At the end of the same month, May 1938, a double band of 30 girls sailed from Newhaven to Dieppe on a French tour which included Brittany, Paris and the coastal resort of La Baule.

In La Baule they gave a combined performance in the Parc des Dryades with drummers of the French 65th Infantry Regiment. The large audience were vocal in their appreciation of the mace-wielding skills of the 16 year-old 'Tambour Major,' Ada Clatworthy (pictured left).

The band returned to France for a five-day visit to Calais in July. On their first evening the band attended a church service conducted by Mr Graves, and the highlight of the following day was a visit to the City Hall. The girls marched, while playing, into the building and up the stairs into the main hall where they were given a formal reception by the Mayor. They performed in various theatres and other venues in and around Calais during their stay, and a memorable moment occurred when Doris Patterson played a solo from the lighthouse balcony.

As 1938 progressed, the international situation worsened. Hitler's Germany had annexed Austria in March, and was now casting its eyes at the Sudetenland area of Czechoslovakia. In June the Dagenham girls undertook two engagements highlighting the sacrifices of the previous war. First they

The band inside Calais Town Hall, 1938 *(Dagenham Girl Pipers Veterans' Association)*

appeared in their regular slot in the annual memorial parade at East Ham in memory of 16 year-old John Travers ('Jack') Cornwell, who had been awarded a posthumous Victoria Cross for his heroism during the naval Battle of Jutland in 1916. The same month the band marched to the Cenotaph in Whitehall to perform during a service conducted by the Dean of Westminster.

The following month, July 1938, a double band of 30 girls played at Wembley Stadium as part of an international co-operative festival. The crowd numbered over 70,000, their biggest audience yet. The band were led by Edith Turnbull, and premiered a bagpipe medley *Song tunes of the nations,* arranged by her. The undoubted highlight of the latter part of 1938 for Edith and the band was being invited to take part in the Royal Command Performance, held at the London Coliseum in November in the presence of King George VI and Queen Elizabeth. The Queen (later Queen Elizabeth the Queen Mother) was the daughter of the Earl of Strathmore and had been brought up at Glamis Castle in Scotland. She was to prove a staunch supporter of the band.

Early in 1939 Mr Graves vested financial control of the band into a limited company. Previously he had carried the responsibility himself, but with an ambitious American tour in the offing he decided, with local support, to set the organization on a more businesslike footing.

Plans for the American visit had been under way since October the previous year. In connection with it the girls had to have a medical, and at the next band practice Mr Graves told them the doctor had said they were so fit there was no reason why they shouldn't live to the year 2000. As Lily Vale recalled, 'We all hooted with laughter at the thought of being old ladies, but Mr Graves suggested we make plans for meeting then, and the Pledge was drawn up'.

The band outside the Dagenham Civic Centre in 1938, the year their Millennium pledge was first made (*LBBD Archives at Valence House*)

The pledge was signed by 53 members on 21 October 1938, and subsequently sworn by all new recruits. The wording was as follows:

> We, the undersigned members of the Dagenham Girl Pipers, desire to place on record our appreciation of our present physical fitness, and to pledge ourselves to avoid at all times in the future, any habits that, in our individual judgement, would interfere with the enjoyment of perfect good health. We desire so to live, now and in the coming years, that we may take to our old age a sound and healthy body. And, in the hope that we may be spared to that old age, we now promise that if possible and convenient, we who now sign this document will meet for a reunion of the Dagenham Girl Pipers at whatever building is then the Civic Centre Headquarters in Dagenham, at noon on January 1st, 2000 AD.

In April 1939 25 girls, led by Edith Turnbull and accompanied by the band's assistant manager Mr H.W. Morrison, (father of the piper and accompanist Beatrice Morrison), stepped on board the *SS American Trader* at the Royal Albert Docks for a ten-day voyage across the Atlantic. They would play in the British Amusement Section of the New York World's Fair for six months, followed by a tour of Canada. The World's Fair covered an area of over 1,200 acres and would be attended by about 26 million people. In the words of Alfred Haynes: 'Besides enabling the band to play its melodies and airs in a second continent, the contract gave conclusive proof that the Pipers had reached the status of a top-ranking entertainment team'.

The girls lived at Long Island, and each day travelled to the 'Merrie England' area of the Fair, containing mock-ups of buildings such as the Globe Theatre and the Old Curiosity Shop. It had a 'village green' on which the band

The band appearing in the 'Merrie England' section of the New York World's Fair in 1939.
(above, LBBD Archives at Valence House;
below, Dagenham Girl Pipers Veterans' Association)

performed seven times a day. They also made regular radio broadcasts. On 10 June King George VI and Queen Elizabeth visited the Fair, and the band marked their arrival by playing 'All the blue bonnets are over the Border' and 'Cock o' the North'.

Ford Motor Company had an exhibition hall at the Fair, and because of the company's association with Dagenham the band were a natural choice to play there. Henry Ford himself heard them one day, and then asked them back to tea with him and his family. He also invited them to visit the company's headquarters in Detroit, Michigan. Coincidentally, on the very same day, back in England Peggy Iris was leading a band performing at the Ford Gymkhana at Brooklands in Surrey.

Peggy and her band had just returned after spending a week at the International Exhibition at Liége, Belgium, which was opened by King Leopold III of the Belgians. A memorable feature of this trip was the saga of the baby black-footed goat presented to the band as a mascot by the Mayor of Liége. The goat won the hearts of all the girls, so they were naturally very upset when it was impounded by customs officials at Dover. Sadly no amount of phone calls to Whitehall by Mr Graves could convince them free the goat, which was soon sent back to Belgium.

The huge success of the 1937 tour of Germany had led to an invitation for a repeat visit in July 1939. By this time, however, Anglo-German relations had worsened so much that Mr Graves was uncertain about whether to continue with the trip. After much consultation he decided it would go ahead, subject to day-to-day advice from British Consular staff in Germany.

So a band of 15 girls, led by Peggy Iris and accompanied by Mr Graves, spent a month touring 25 towns in the Black Forest and Taunus areas of South-West

Germany. On the face of it things were going perfectly. They were receiving enthusiastic receptions and staying with friendly local families rather than in hotels. Yet behind the scenes the warnings from British diplomats grew more and more urgent.

On 5 August 1939 Mr Graves was told in no uncertain terms that war was inevitable, and that if the band were still in Germany when it happened, they might well be detained indefinitely in an internment camp. The band had by this time reached Friedrichshafen, on the northern side of the Bodensee (Lake Constance), near the borders with Austria and Switzerland.

The following morning, the band marched as planned to the railway station and boarded a train. It was not, however, the one they were due to take. Mr Graves had decided to terminate the tour and set the party on the long journey back to Britain via Kehl, Strasbourg, Brussels, Ostend and finally Dover. War broke out four weeks later.

Chapter 3
Wartime & the 1940s

At 11am on Sunday 3 September 1939 the Prime Minister, Neville Chamberlain, announced that Britain was now at war with Germany. That very morning, the band were at a London cinema ready to rehearse for a week of performances with Billy Cotton and his band. They listened to the announcement on the radio, took cover soon afterwards when an air raid siren sounded (thankfully, a false alarm) and returned to Dagenham knowing the shows were cancelled and the future uncertain. All places where crowds might gather and be at risk of enemy action, such as cinemas, theatres and music halls, were immediately closed down by the authorities.

With all its bookings now cancelled, the company running the band had insufficient financial reserves to continue employing the 28 full-timers on its books. Also, women would be needed to work in factories, offices and on the land to support the war effort and take the place of men called up for active service. Newspapers jumped to the conclusion that the band was no more. A *Times* headline proclaimed 'Dagenham Girl Pipers: Famous Players Disbanded'. This was not true, as we shall see, but the media's concern demonstrated how well-known and well-loved the band had become.

Mr Graves happened to be on holiday when the crisis occurred. On returning he gave an interview to *The Times*, protesting that 'there ought to be some little place for a band like this, which is nationally and internationally famous, to fill in wartime. We have often played at camps, and were always very popular with the soldiers'. The paper's editorial agreed, declaring that the band was 'an early war casualty on the Home Front...the blow will be deeply deplored, not only in Dagenham, which has always been proud of its unique band, but also far afield'. Little did anyone know that the war, far from destroying the band, would lead to them being busier and more renowned than ever.

Mr Graves had to turn his attention to the girls in North America, who had been performing at the Canadian National Exhibition at Lake Ontario when war broke out. Should they be brought straight home? This would put their lives at risk, as German U-Boats were already sinking ships in the Atlantic. Eventually, after consultation with the girls' parents, it was decided that they would return in two sections. A group of 14 younger band members would leave in the middle of October. The remainder, led by Edith Turnbull, would remain to fulfil contracts in Canada and the USA.

The junior girls accordingly set sail on the *SS Washington*. Lily Vale, then 16, recalls that:

> Our chaperone and members of the crew reassured us that all would be well. We had plenty of lifeboat drill as a daily routine. During the 8 to 9 days of the journey we were kept well occupied with band practice and joined in with the other activities on deck. We were not made aware of the danger and threats surrounding our journey until we reached home, when we heard of the anxiety experienced by our parents.

They arrived in Southampton after what had been, to everyone's relief, an uneventful voyage. Mr Graves declared: 'These girls are heroines. They are only the junior section of the band in America, yet they defied the menace of the German submarines while thousands of adults are staying in America because they are afraid to go to sea'. Their names were placed on a band Roll of Honour: Patricia Arnold, Margaret Fraser, Selina Lee, Alma Payne, Ilene Reynolds, Elsie Roast, Marguerite Sergeant, Lily Sims, Ivy Spooner, Elsie Tarling, Eileen Townley, Lily Vale, Joan White and Margaret Williams.

Four months later, in February 1940, the senior girls also returned safely, and a Welcome Home party was held for them at Raydons House. The newcomers had much to tell their colleagues. There had been, for example, the memorable occasion in November 1939 when they had been invited to the White House by America's First Lady, Mrs Eleanor Roosevelt. The following day they had been received by the British Ambassador, and on Armistice Day had been given the honour of parading with the American Legion to Washington's war memorial.

The story of the band's many and varied activities during World War Two could fill a book in itself, and the 1945 booklet *Piping through the War* gives a detailed account. It explains that the band fell into four distinct groupings during this time. (Some girls, of course, switched between them as the war progressed). The groups were:

- The Home Band, engaged in full-time war work and giving their spare time, chiefly weekends and evenings, to the band. Examples of the kind of work its members undertook are: in factories, offices, the Food Office and National Fire Service, Air Raid Precautions (ARP), Women's Land Army (WLA), Women's Voluntary Services (WVS), ambulance drivers, nurses and telephone operators.
- Girls who had entered the Forces (the ATS, WRNS and WAAF)
- Girls undertaking full-time band work, usually under the auspices of ENSA (Entertainments National Service Association). They were

known as the Touring Band and, later, as the bands multiplied, as Touring Band 1, Touring Band 2 etc.

- Finally, there were the younger girls still at school, many of whom became evacuees. Those remaining in Dagenham continued to attend regular training classes and parades.

The Home Band

Women and girls in the Dagenham area were in demand for war work in local offices and factories such as Fords (which produced thousands of Army vehicles), Sterling (armaments) and May & Baker (medical supplies). Mr Graves and Edith Turnbull both undertook clerical work at Fords.

Other members of the band joined the Women's Land Army, set up to replace male farm workers who had left for active service. Keeping up food production was of the utmost importance to keep the population from starving, as U-boat activity had caused food imports to dwindle.

Mr and Mrs Graves's thatched cottage at Great Sampford in the Essex countryside was ideally placed to accommodate girls wishing to join the Land Army. The *Dagenham Post* of 12 July 1940 reported that 'This week three prominent members [of the band] have started work on the land and are employed on a farm near Saffron Walden. The latest report is to the effect that they are succeeding well at their new work and finding it very interesting'. They camped in chalets in the garden as they did when attending summer Piping School as youngsters. In their uniforms of brown corduroy breeches, knee-length woollen socks, green pullovers and beige shirts, girls got to work on the vitally important task of helping the nation to be self-sufficient in food production.

The closure of places of entertainment was judged to be an over-reaction, and they were soon allowed to reopen. As well as raising morale on the Home

Three band members in the Women's Land Army: Grace Richards (left), Margaret Fraser (centre) and Ada Clatworthy *(Dagenham Girl Pipers Veterans' Association)*

Front, they would be used to stage fund-raising events for the war effort and war charities. Television broadcasts remained suspended (TV was a rarity then in British homes anyway) so cinemas were also used for wartime public information films and newsreels.

So the opportunity now arose, as Mr Graves knew it would, for the band to step back into action. The girls were, of course, part-time, and given just expenses instead of regular wages, but their commitment and quality of performance remained unchanged. Behind the scenes, they planned and rehearsed new tunes and scenes to echo the patriotic spirit of the time.

The band's first wartime engagement came in November 1939, at the opening of a Granada cinema at Kingston-upon-Thames. Their medleys of wartime tunes were enthusiastically received, and the finale was sensational. As the band played *There'll always be an England* the scenery moved aside to reveal Drum Major Ada Clatworthy, mace held high, standing on a replica Nelson's Column. The thunderous cheers could be heard in the streets outside.

More cinema engagements followed in and around London, and the band also travelled further afield. In December 1939, for example, they appeared at an Auxiliary Fire Service concert in a cinema in Swindon, Wiltshire, in which they played a medley of *Song Tunes from many Wars* including pieces from the American Civil War, the Boer War, World War One and the new tunes of the current war.

In March 1940 a burst of publicity surrounded Edith Turnbull's 21st birthday, and the following month saw the publication of her biography, *A famous English girl* by Frank Craske.

Later that year the Blitz began in earnest, but the band were determined to honour their bookings. The *Dagenham Post* told its readers in August that while travelling to and from the Hackney Empire the girls had to leave their coach several times and head for the nearest air raid shelter. The grateful audience, which included the Home Secretary, Herbert Morrison, rewarded them with 'a splendid reception,' and Mr Morrison shook hands with them.

The following month the *Post's* headline declared 'The true English Spirit – Dagenham Girl Pipers unperturbed'. It related how, after the band had given two shows at the Dagenham British Legion Hall and were enjoying a refreshment break, the air raid sirens sounded and they dashed to a nearby shelter, taking their lemonade and cake with them. After the All Clear came, the girls took their places on stage and defiantly played *There'll always be an England* to an empty hall. 'Truly an illustration of the spirit that England both needs and possesses today!' commented the *Post*. The band's advertisements also displayed a confidence in the future, by seeking priority bookings for victory celebrations!

The growing list of organizations aided by the Home Band included National Savings, the Red Cross, Wings for Victory, the Merchant Navy and the

Holidays at Home campaign. In acknowledgement of their work, they were invited in summer 1943 to take part in a large parade at Windsor Castle before the Royal Family. Of the twelve bands present, theirs was the only civilian and the only girls' band.

A complete change of scene occurred elsewhere in 1943 when the girls appeared in the film *The Dummy Talks*. The plot centred on the murder of a ventriloquist, and coincidentally also featured the all-female jazz band the Ivy Benson Band. Formed in 1940 as Ivy Benson and her Rhythm Girls for the *Meet the Girls* revue, it joined the Girl Pipers in pioneering women's participation in traditionally male fields of entertainment. In October that year the band celebrated its 13th birthday. At the anniversary party Mr Graves declared that the band was 'now stronger, better and bigger than ever before'.

January 1944 saw the Home Band performing at Forces House at Ilford in the presence of a contingent of US troops. Their programme included tunes adapted from popular American songs as a compliment to them. In March

Entertaining American troops during the war *(LBBD Archives at Valence House)*

1944 the girls took a prominent part in the Salute the Soldier campaign tour, giving many performances in the London area. They played a new *Salute the Soldier march* composed by Allan Cameron, one of their previous Pipe Majors.

That same year, 1944, saw the wedding of their first home-grown Pipe Major, Edith Turnbull. She had first seen New Yorker Charles Kawa back in 1939 at the World's Fair. They met again when Charles was posted to England as a Staff Sergeant in the US Air Force, and married in September 1944 at Osborne Hall, the ceremony performed by Mr Graves. On leaving the church, the newlyweds walked through an avenue of Girl Pipers and American airmen. So many people surged forward to catch a glimpse of them that the *Dagenham Post* photographer had to take refuge in the bridal car to escape being crushed!

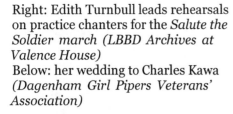

Right: Edith Turnbull leads rehearsals on practice chanters for the *Salute the Soldier march (LBBD Archives at Valence House)*
Below: her wedding to Charles Kawa *(Dagenham Girl Pipers Veterans' Association)*

The same month Drum Major Florrie Kenningale also married an American serviceman, Lieutenant James Hart. Florrie left the band immediately, but for Edith it would be business as usual for the time being. Usually, band life, with its long tours and busiest times at Christmas, New Year and Bank Holidays, made it impossible for girls to even think of staying on once they married. Yet in wartime the situation changed. Edith and several other girls remained in the band while their husbands returned to active service.

Armed services

Meanwhile, other members of the band had joined the Armed Services. Women were not allowed to actually bear arms, but undertook a wide range of support duties within the Army, Navy and Air Force. The relevant wing of the Army was the Auxiliary Territorial Service (ATS). Its members wore khaki uniforms and did driving, cooking, clerical work, staffed anti-aircraft establishments or were trained in trades such as carpentry and welding. It comes as no surprise to learn that Dagenham Girl Pipers played a crucial role in forming the highly-regarded ATS Military Band.

Comparable organizations within the other services were the Women's Royal Naval Service (WRNS, known as Wrens) and the Women's Auxiliary Air Force (WAAF), whose members helped staff radar stations and maintain and fly barrage balloons.

ENSA (Entertainments National Service Association) and other wartime variety shows

In March 1941 the band signed its first ENSA contract, for a piper and drummer to be part of a show called *Knightsbridge Parade*. The connection grew until several separate units of the band were employed full-time by ENSA, travelling with concert parties entertaining troops the length and

The band's ENSA, CSEU and wartime variety shows included *Wise & Otherwise* (above) and *Desert Rats* (right) *(Jean Vale)*

breadth of the country. These shows included *On Parade* and *Piping Hot*. Band members also took part in similar variety shows run independently of ENSA, such as *Best Foot Forward* (with their old friend the singer and comedian Will Fyffe), and *Wise and Otherwise,* run by Ernie and Renee Shannon. Jean Vale took part in several wartime productions, and recalls that:

> ENSA parties were always billeted in ENSA hostels, usually big country houses surrounded with large grounds and staffed by NAAFI personnel. Many of the amusing episodes that we were involved in came from the tales the NAAFI girls told us about the houses being haunted...We were

taken to a different camp each evening by coach unless it was a very large camp and then we would appear for several nights there. We were usually given a supper after the show either in the officers' mess or the sergeants' mess...When we played at Air Force camps it was not unusual for crews to be called out for missions during the show. Often when we left the camp they had not yet all returned and that would disturb us. We were very young to be dealing with this.

After the war some girls took part in productions for the CSEU (Combined Services Entertainment Unit), which had replaced ENSA. These shows included *Desert Rats* and *Scots Wha Hae*.

With ENSA in Africa

In April 1942 Pipe Major Peggy Iris, then 22, and 18 year-old Sergeant Margaret Fraser left for Africa and the Middle East under the auspices of ENSA. Peggy had always longed to visit Africa, and using transport ranging from trains and planes to cars and camels, she and Margaret undertook an extraordinary journey. As the *Dagenham Post* commented on their return nearly three years later, 'Their adventures, if ever written fully, would make more exciting reading than many a modern thriller'.

Initially with a 10-strong concert party called the Globe Trotters, and later with ENSA Follies, they entertained troops in 15 countries including the Sudan, Kenya, Uganda, Madagascar, Egypt, Syria, Libya and Tunisia. They arrived in Cairo in October 1942 shortly before the Battle of El Alamein began, and in the summer of 1943 were in Tripoli, where General Montgomery heard them at a garrison theatre. He spoke to the girls after the show, praising their playing and thanking them for their role in boosting the morale of the troops. The pair gave over 1000 shows, insisting on wearing their full uniforms

Some Egyptian scenes
from the travels of Peggy
Iris & Margaret Fraser
(Peggy Iris)

despite the often intense heat and humidity. When Peggy and Margaret returned to England in February 1945, a crowd including the Mayor of Dagenham welcomed them on the platform at Dagenham Heathway Station. They were afterwards awarded the Africa Star, given for service in the North African campaign.

The end of the war

After almost six years of war, 1945 saw peace at last, with VE Day (surrender of the German forces in Europe) on 8 May, followed by VJ Day (victory over Japan) on 15 August.

At that time the band was appearing at the London Palladium in *Happy and Glorious*, which ran for 18 months and also starred Tommy Trinder, Arthur Askey, Vera Lynn, Eddie Gray, Will Hay and Jack Hylton. On the night of 4 May 1945, with victory in Europe in sight, the nine girls currently performing in *Happy and Glorious* were taken by coach to Windsor Castle after the show together with Mr Graves. As part of a special entertainment before the Royal Family, they performed their act from the show alongside comedian Tommy Trinder.

Afterwards the girls enjoyed supper in the magnificent State Dining Room and had the opportunity of speaking to the King and Queen. When the King was told that some people objected to the band wearing Royal Stewart Tartan, he replied that the girls were welcome to tell anyone who complained that he himself 'had no objection!'

(Author's collection)

Backstage with singer Elisabeth Welch (left) and comedian Tommy Trinder (above) during the run of *Happy and Glorious* at the London Palladium *(Bette Read)*

On VE Day itself, the Home Band were performing at a US Air Force base in East Anglia. To round off their wartime achievements, they took part in many Victory Week Parades around the country, marching alongside Service bands.

October 1945 saw the band's own 15th anniversary celebration. At a party in St George's Church Hall, Mr Graves declared that the past year had been their busiest ever, and that as the band had now visited 25 countries it was 'the only band that can really claim to be international'. This slogan 'The Dagenham

VE Day. Unusually, Pipe Majors Peggy Iris (left) and Edith Turnbull (centre) are pictured together. Normally they would be leading different bands *(Dagenham Girl Pipers Veterans' Association)*

Girl Pipers – the International Band', alongside an image of the globe, would become a permanent fixture on the band's publicity and stationery in the years to come.

Towards the end of 1945 the lavishly-illustrated booklet *Piping through the War* went on sale at 2s 6d. It was edited by Ivor Halstead, who declared in the foreword that 'It is not difficult to imagine how our serving men and women, cut off from home in lonely encampments in Britain and abroad, have welcomed the sight of the fresh and happy faces of the Girl Pipers and the sound of the music they bring alive with the idiom of the native heath'.

The cover of *Piping through the War* bore a portrait of Edith Turnbull, but, sadly for the band, it was now only a matter of time before she left for a new life in the USA. In February 1946 Edith departed on the *Vulcania* with other so-called GI Brides. When the ship docked in New York, Edith appeared in her uniform and piped off her fellow war brides, much to the surprise to her husband waiting at the dockside!

A popular publication of 1945 *(LBBD Archives at Valence House)*

The war may have been over, but the ENSA work continued for some time yet both at home and abroad. Margaret Fraser and Margaret Williams spent six months in the Middle East, including performances on a floating stage at Suez fashioned out of a tank landing craft. These shows were for ex-Japanese prisoners of war now on their way home.

Peggy Iris, meanwhile, led a band of six in an ENSA show called *More the Merrier*, first to Europe and later to India and Ceylon. They were one of the first groups to enter Germany after the fall of Berlin, and experienced the

In Berlin, 1945.
Right, with local children *(Peggy Iris)*; below, a street parade *(LBBD Archives at Valence House)*

devastation of the ruined cities, the horror of the Belsen concentration camp and a session of the Nuremburg war crimes trials.

Following a short break in England over the New Year of 1946, the *More the Merrier* concert party then took the four-week voyage to Bombay (now Mumbai). By May 1946 they had reached Ceylon (now Sri Lanka). Walter Newman, a former *Dagenham Post* employee now serving in the Royal Navy, wrote of the impression made by the band at a concert in a camp set in the heart of the jungle:

Long-distance travels in 1946: in India (left); with rickshaws in Ceylon (below)
(LBBD Archives at Valence House)

Into this strange – and somewhat eerie – setting they brought a touch of the old country. To the Scots they brought fond memories of the Highlands, and to the boys from Dagenham they brought – home...the sprawling camp of bamboo huts echoes to the notes of a Scottish reel. For a few minutes those who had been away for the weary war years were able to savour memories of home.

The party arrived back in England in September 1946 after a year's absence. In Ceylon Margaret Fraser had re-encountered Noel Dyson Rooke, a tea planter and former Navy officer she had first met in Suez nine months previously. The couple were to marry in 1947.

In the meantime, the rest of the band enjoyed in the summer of 1946 what Mr Graves described as its busiest period ever. He was now managing the band from an office in Craven Street, near Charing Cross in London. Its engagements at that time included leading the carnival parade of the first-ever

The band leading the Dagenham British Legion on a march-past before the King &Queen outside Buckingham Palace in 1946, marking the first anniversary of the end of the war
(LBBD Archives at Valence House)

Three Towns Show, which took place in Hornchurch and was run jointly by Hornchurch, Dagenham and Romford. It was the forerunner of the famous Dagenham Town Show, which began in 1952.

The pipers hit the silver screen again with the film *School for Secrets*, directed by and starring Peter Ustinov. It concerned a group of British scientists working to develop the first radar system in time for it to be used in the Battle of Britain. A band of 20 girls, led by Sergeant Hilda Creffield, were seen playing at a victory parade. The scene was filmed at Bournemouth, and included a young Bill Owen (later to achieve TV fame as Compo in *Last of the Summer Wine*) as an American airman.

Dancing with Bill Owen in the 1946 film *School for Secrets*
(Dagenham Girl Pipers Veterans' Association)

Performing at the Hague, 1946 *(LBBD Archives at Valence House)*

Two European tours also took place that summer of 1946. A band left Harwich in June on the *Scandinavian* for a three-month tour of Sweden, led by Pipe Major Marshall and Staff Sergeant Elsie Spooner. Just two weeks after its return, another group of girls (including seven of the party who had been to Sweden) set off for a seven-week tour of Holland, including visits to the Hague, Rotterdam and Amsterdam.

In June 1946 the band carried out an engagement in Woodford, the constituency of Winston Churchill, Britain's wartime Prime Minister, and met the great man himself. In her book *One of a Kind: notes on memoirs of a Pied Piper*, Margaret ('Mickey') Child recalls that 'we were introduced with handshakes all round. I still remember the faint aroma of whisky and cigar smoke as he passed by!'

A band played in Manchester Town Square to welcome in the New Year of 1947. They were in Manchester for a lengthy engagement at the famous Belle Vue Circus, in an entertainment park which included a zoo, amusement park and speedway circuit.

In March 1947, a full band left for a three-week tour of the North of England on behalf of the British Sailors' Society. Their opening performance was at Newcastle United Football Club's ground on 22 March. The tour also included a visit to Alnwick Castle as guests of the Duchess of Northumberland, who later attended the band's concert at Alnwick Town Hall. After dates in Hull, Leeds and the West Riding of Yorkshire, the final weekend was occupied by visits to Butlins holiday camps at Filey and Skegness. In the early summer the band returned to Skegness for a week, giving daily outdoor and indoor displays and street marches.

In March 1947 it was announced that one of the band's most well-known personalities, its leading bass drummer, Elsie Spooner, was to leave for Canada to marry Len McOuatt, a former sergeant in the Canadian Army. Elsie had been in the band for nearly 15 years, and had starred at the London Palladium for 18 months in *Happy and Glorious*.

The band pictured in Skegness, 1947 *(Dagenham Girl Pipers Veterans' Association)*

Early in 1947, a band of 10 left for a tour of France with the circus Cirque Amar. They slept in a converted railway carriage which was taken off the rails and towed to each site the circus stopped at. In *One of a kind*, Mickey Child remembered that:

> We did a short show at each performance while the lions' cage was being erected. Once over, we made a hasty retreat as the lions bounded into the ring!...Another deviation from our piping and dancing was 'dressing the stage' for the snake charmers act as they came on...We were provided with coloured silk baggy pants and voluminous blouses topped off with yashmaks. We all beat another hasty retreat before the snakes reared their heads!

Beginning at Marseilles, the band performed at resorts along the Riviera, including Monte Carlo, before travelling to Paris. Here they were introduced to General de Gaulle, who had come to see the show. After touring the northern French coast the circus wound its way back to Marseilles. The

Leaving their railway carriage accommodation in France
(LBBD Archives at Valence House)

In Paris, 1947: at the Place de la Concorde (above); and on stage (below)
(LBBD Archives at Valence House)

journey was due to continue in North Africa, but this was cancelled at the last minute – not before the instruments, uniforms and baggage had sailed to Tunis! Altogether the French tour had lasted some eight months.

The Royal Command Performance, 1947: rehearsal of the grand finale (above) and programme (top right) *(Dagenham Girl Pipers Veterans' Association)*

Right: Meeting Oliver Hardy after the show *(LBBD Archives at Valence House)*

The undoubted highlight of 1947 for the band was their appearance at the Royal Command Performance on 3 November at the London Palladium in the presence of the King, Queen and Princesses Elizabeth and Margaret. The band was invited at the special request of the Queen, who, as we have seen, was one of their strongest supporters. A massed band of 60 took to the stage in a segment called 'Among the heather and hills,' appearing with Robert Wilson, (known as the 'Voice of Scotland') and Scottish brother and sister entertainers Vic and Joe Crastonian. The girls reappeared for the finale, *There's no Business like Show Business,* with the whole company, including Laurel and Hardy, Tommy Trinder and Gracie Fields.

Alongside a tour bus in the 1940s *(Dagenham Girl Pipers Veterans' association)*

The Christmas and New Year period of 1947-48 saw the band appearing in the pantomime *Red Riding Hood* at the Wimbledon Theatre. A Highland scene had been specially created for them. The show also starred legendary music hall artiste Tessie O'Shea, Jacqueline Boyle (as the heroine), and popular radio comedian Reg Dixon, who was known for his signature tune *Confidentially* and the catchphrase 'I'm not well, I'm proper poorly!'

In stage and circus shows, the band were now regularly supplementing the chorus as well as performing their own act. In *Red Riding Hood*, some of them bravely agreed to do a flying ballet scene. Unfortunately, on one occasion one girl got caught up in the high wire, and was eventually folded up into the curtain as it closed around her!

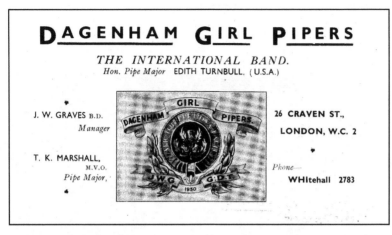

A letterhead of 1947
(LBBD Archives at Valence House)

Early in 1948 the band were at Marylebone Studios filming a segment of *Dick Barton: special agent*, based on the popular daily radio serial. In the film, the hero battled a ring of Nazi spies planning to poison London's water supply.

In September of that year, 1948, Hilda Creffield and Eileen Townley were both appointed to the rank of Pipe Major. October saw the band's 18th birthday. The Heathway was brought to a standstill by a tremendous parade of nearly 60 girls, headed by three Drum Majors, marching to the band's original home at Osborne Square.

The celebrations were, however, overshadowed by the shock announcement by Mr Graves, now 67, that he had decided to retire. A few days later he wrote a letter to each of the girls, ending with:

> ...When I spoke last Friday night I was too upset to say one word more than the prepared statement. There was very much I wanted to say. Let this brief letter convey to each of you an assurance of my quite unchanged affection and regard. No one will ever take your place in my thoughts and memory. God bless you individually. God bless our wonderful band...Thank you for all the past lovely years.
>
> Your friend, J.W. Graves.

The *Dagenham Post* of 20 October 1948 reported that:

> The founder, Mr J.W. Graves, has retired from the management and control of the Dagenham Girl Pipers. The position will now be held jointly by Pipe Major Peggy Iris and Pipe Major T.K. Marshall, MVO. Making this announcement, the London office of the Pipers stated that Mr Graves would still be associated with the band in an advisory capacity...Mr Graves told a reporter: 'I am getting older and my health has not been too good. We thought it best that I should pass the work on to someone else rather then, perhaps, have to do it suddenly later on'.

Shortly afterwards, Peggy Iris and Pipe Major Marshall asked Mr David Land to join them on the band's management team. Mr Land had been born in Whitechapel in East London in May 1918, of Polish Jewish ancestry. After a spell as a draper's assistant in Dagenham's Broad Street Market, he had first ventured into business in 1938 with a hardware shop there. He entered the Royal Army Service Corps at the outbreak of war. Mr Land told the *Barking Advertiser* in 1977 that: 'While serving in the Army, I fell in love with show business. I began organizing entertainments for the troops, acting as Master of Ceremonies for camp variety shows, and talent-spotting amongst the Tommies'. After the war he extended his interests in the Dagenham area to include a chain of nine hardware shops, a pawnshop and a property business.

Yet at the same time Mr Land was pursuing his show business interests by founding a theatrical agency in Broad Street. He was soon organizing charity concerts in Barking, Dagenham and Ilford, featuring well-known local performers such as Vera Lynn, the Forces' Sweetheart (who was living at that time with her mother in Upney Lane, Barking) and Max Bygraves (who, after being demobbed from the RAF in 1945, had settled in Central Park Avenue in Dagenham before moving to Thorntons Farm Avenue, Rush Green).

Left, Peggy Iris & Pipe Major Marshall *(Ken & Richard Chapman collection)*;
Above, David Land with some of the band in 1953 *(the David Land Agency)*

Mr Land had often used the Dagenham Girl Pipers in his concerts, and had developed close ties with the organization. Their 18th birthday celebrations had seen the introduction of a trophy (later to be known as the Graves Cup) presented by Mrs Land in memory of her brother, RAF Flying Officer Harold Brook Levinson. It was to be awarded to the girl judged to have the most outstanding record of achievement over the year.

David Land's other show business connections at that time included Stanley Black, a neighbour from the early days in Whitechapel. He was now conductor of the BBC Dance Orchestra, which gave radio broadcasts most evenings, and would become one of the best-known names in British music. Mr Black came to Dagenham in November 1948 as a guest at band practice in St George's Hall in Rogers Road. The following year Mr Land secured for the band the use of the much larger Drill Hall in Halbutt Street, home of the local Territorial Army battalion.

In January 1949 the band were a natural choice to appear at the local premiere of a big screen epic with a Scottish theme, *Bonnie Prince Charlie*. Directed by Alexander Korda, it starred David Niven as the Prince and Margaret Leighton as Flora Macdonald, the girl who helped him escape after the failed Jacobite rebellion. The event took place at the Princess Cinema in New Road, Dagenham, opposite the Ford factory.

The band ready to perform at a cinema *(the David Land Agency)*

Mr and Mrs Graves were now living in their country cottage at Great Sampford, and in March 1949 the Mayor of Dagenham travelled there to perform the official opening of a Dagenham Girl Pipers museum and picture gallery in the cottage. The exhibits included many and varied souvenirs of the band's travels at home and abroad. When Mr and Mrs Graves celebrated their silver wedding in May that year, they received a large number of gifts and telegrams from all over the country. Later that year, though, they made the decision to leave Essex and set up home near Sittingbourne in Mr Graves's native county of Kent.

As the band's 19th anniversary approached in October, they had a stroke of luck when Mr A.G. Smith, managing director of the large Bartons' Bakery in Kemp Road, Dagenham, happened to hear the band play at the Park Lane Hotel. Mr Smith was so impressed that he offered to donate a special birthday cake for the band. It weighed a colossal 60lbs, took a week to bake, and was surmounted by a doll dressed as a Piper. In her speech at the anniversary gathering, Peggy Iris said that history had been made that summer when three bands had performed every day for a week. 'This year', she told the girls, 'you have made our name greater than ever before'.

Chapter 4
The 1950s

The band continued to be busy during the winter of 1949-50, with units performing in several pantomimes, such as *Cinderella* in South Wales and a touring production of *Red Riding Hood* in the south of England.

In March 1950 a small band travelled to Paris to play in conjunction with film *The Swordsmen*. Two months later Arsenal won the FA Cup, and two young Pipers were on hand at their home ground, Highbury, to carry the trophy as the team enjoyed a victory parade.

In October 1950 the band celebrated another milestone – their 20th anniversary. A special service took place at Dagenham Parish Church, during which their instruments were re-dedicated and a celebratory Plain Bob Minor peal of 1260 changes rung by seven bellringers. Bartons Bakeries once again provided a beautiful cake, which weighed nearly half a hundredweight and had a top in the shape of a drum with pipes lying on it. BBC Radio Light Programme listeners heard Stanley Black give a message of congratulations during his programme *Top Score*.

In the following year, 1951, the Festival of Britain was held. The centrepiece was on the south bank of the Thames, with attractions including the Royal Festival Hall and an amusement park containing the iconic Skylon. Communities throughout Britain also staged their own Festival events that summer, and the band notched up an astonishing 170 Festival of Britain engagements in London and elsewhere. They appeared in many venues in their home borough, such as Valence Park, St Chad's Park and Central Park, and also starred in the main Dagenham Carnival procession on 30 June.

In July 1951 the band were playing at the Sandringham Estate Cottage Horticultural Show when King George VI and Queen Elizabeth arrived unexpectedly, called for chairs and remained for the rest of the performance. It was the first time the girls had been the sole entertainers for the King and Queen, who sent a message afterwards saying how much they'd enjoyed the performance.

That same month saw the band leave from Tilbury Docks for a two-month tour of Sweden and Finland. Hilda Creffield was in charge of a party of seven girls. The band had not been to Finland before, and it became 28th on the list of nations they had visited.

As the band's 21st anniversary approached, Mr Graves was welcomed back to Osborne Hall on 2 September 1951 to officiate at the marriage of 20 year-old Drum Major Jackie Molinsky to West End theatre producer Andy Thewlis. That evening Mr Graves gave the sermon at Osborne Hall.

On 6 October the band held its coming-of-age party at the Drill Hall. Bartons had once more produced an impressive two-tier cake, which Peggy Iris cut with a claymore. The guests danced to the music of Syd Payne and his orchestra. A poignant speech was given by Dagenham's mayor, Mr Joseph Hollidge, who

Drum Major Jackie Molinsky
(Author's collection)

74

Peggy Iris cutting the band's 21st birthday cake *(LBBD Archives at Valence House)*

spoke about his daughter Grace, who had joined the band at the age of 12 but had died only six years later. The following day a parade and special service was held at Dagenham Parish Church, followed by a march-past in Old Dagenham Park at which the salute was taken by the Lord Lieutenant of Essex, Colonel Sir Francis Whitmore.

That same month the band began another tour of Germany, which proved so successful that it was extended by five weeks. It began in the north-western port city of Bremen, where the band appeared on stage at the Astoria. Before leaving Bremen the girls visited a car factory, where three vehicles just off the assembly line had been prepared for them to use in a parade around the city. Thousands of people lined the streets to cheer the band and present them with flowers.

Back home in Dagenham, the Pipers continued to appear at the many local cinemas that hosted regular variety shows as well as films. In December 1951, for example, Drum Major Winnie Pile was at the Odeon Whalebone Lane to cut its 18th birthday cake with her ceremonial sword. The band had played at the cinema's official opening in 1933, when it was known as the Mayfair.

On 6 February 1952 the country was shocked to hear that King George VI had died aged only 56. For the Pipers it was especially sad news, as the King had heard them perform many times, was never short of praise and, as we have seen, had even approved their use of the Royal Stuart tartan. The band played the lament *Flowers of the Forest* at a local memorial service for the late King, and joined the Mayor on the steps of the Civic Centre as he read the proclamation of the accession of the young Queen Elizabeth II.

The band at the Civic Centre for the proclamation of the Queen's accession in 1952
(LBBD Archives at Valence House)

In July that year a group of the younger band members, average age 13, travelled to Schwenningen in Germany to display their Highland dancing skills in an international folk dancing competition. They won first prize, an elaborate clock. The same month the band visited the Scottish Highlands for the first time in 15 years.

It had been a long time, too, since the band had visited the USA – since the World's Fair in 1939, in fact. There was accordingly much excitement when it became known that a band of ten would travel to New York in October 1952. They sailed on the *SS Britannic*, and were provided with stylish coats, berets, shoes and handbags to wear while off-duty, sponsored by British

On the liner to New York in October 1952 *(the Barking & Dagenham Post)*

manufacturers. Awaiting them at the quayside at New York was former Pipe Major Edith Turnbull, who treated them to dinner at her home.

The band appeared at Broadway's Latin Quarter nightclub, followed by a season at Miami Beach in Florida. Their leader during the tour, Drum Major Winnie Pile, reported that if it hadn't been for the need to return home for the Queen's Coronation celebrations in June 1953, they could have toured the USA for years! A highlight of their visit was meeting Eleanor Roosevelt, widow of President F.D. Roosevelt, at the Sheraton Hotel in New York, and presenting her with an illuminated scroll of good wishes from the Mayor of Dagenham.

On Christmas Day 1952 a group of parents entered Mr Land's office in Broad Street, Dagenham, for what was at that time a rare treat – a Trans-Atlantic telephone call. Two of the mothers had never used a telephone before. Each girl had just under half a minute's precious conversation. The following month Mr Land took Christmas gift parcels from the families with him when he flew to New York. In May 1953, when Coronation fever was reaching its height, the band launched an exhibition of British goods at a New York department store, including a replica of the Coronation Chair and its cloth of gold canopy, before travelling home.

Presenting Mrs Eleanor Roosevelt with a scroll from the Mayor of Dagenham
(the David Land Agency)

Having recently paraded on Broadway, the girls were soon doing the same with gusto in the more homely surroundings of St Chad's Park, in Chadwell Heath, pulling four brave male volunteers from the audience into an Eightsome Reel! Another local event was the NALGO Christmas party at the Barking Indoor Baths in East Street, which had a sliding floor across the pool, so that it could be used for meetings and entertainments. For the finale, the band led guests on a quickstep march around the hall.

In August 1953 the tour of the USA and Canada was resumed, with Peggy Iris leading a band of ten sailing on the *Queen Mary*. After performing in cities including Philadelphia, St Louis, New York and Montreal, the group returned home towards the end of the year, only for some of them to leave shortly afterwards on the band's most ambitious venture yet – a year-long trip to Australia.

Preparing to leave for America, August 1953: above, David Land discusses the programme with Pipe Major Peggy Iris; and below, some last-minute packing
(the David Land Agency)

Forming an oriental chorus line in Montreal *(Pat Ryder)*

The ten-member Australian party, led by Peggy Iris, departed on the *Strathaird* on 30 December and broke off their 13,000 mile journey at Colombo in Ceylon (now Sri Lanka) to spend a day with their former colleague Margaret Fraser, now Mrs Dyson Rooke, who piped them ashore.

The ship steamed into Sydney Harbour on 3 February 1954, the band piping on the upper deck on arrival in traditional fashion. The Queen and Prince Philip had arrived the same day on a Commonwealth tour. Three days later the band took part in a Royal Command Performance at the Tivoli Theatre, where they were booked to perform for eight weeks. Peggy Iris remembered that 'We marched smartly to take our positions on each side of the red carpet before the Queen arrived, and we received a tremendous reception from the 20,000 people gathered outside. The radio commentator describing the scene remarked how smart and how wonderful we looked'.

During their stay in Australia the band greeted another well-known figure, Lily Fernella Evans, dubbed 'Mrs Dagenham' by the press, who had been a councillor for many years and served as Mayor of Dagenham during World War Two. A great friend of the Pipers, and donor of the Lily Evans Cup for Dancing, Mrs Evans had even been piped aboard the *Athenic* at Millwall's King George V Dock en route to Australia. She stopped off at Melbourne on her way to Tasmania, where she was to spend two years with her son and daughter.

Peggy Iris (centre) and the band take ship for Australia, December 1953 *(Peggy Iris)*

Playing before the Queen in Sydney, 1954 *(the David Land Agency)*

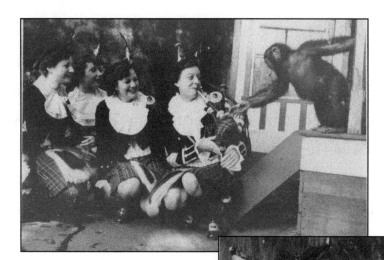

The girls with unusual
audiences in Australia
(*Peggy Iris*)

Readers at home could follow the girls' progress in Australia in the local press. Formal scenes, such as of the band playing at the Shrine of Remembrance in Melbourne, were mixed with snapshots of the girls encountering koalas and kangaroos. The band's Drum Major, Pat Whitworth, also hit the headlines when the *Dagenham Post* revealed that she had 'found romance on the high seas...During the five weeks' cruise, she was introduced to engineer officer William Ryder, and Cupid shot his arrow'. There was more drama for Pat when she collapsed on stage with appendicitis during the tour and had to undergo an emergency operation.

At the Australian War Memorial *(Peggy Iris)*

Several months before the girls returned from Australia in December 1954, another unit of the band had set off yet again to North America for an 18-month coast-to-coast tour. The railway journey from New York to Las Vegas took four days, and Winnie Pile noted that they could see the glittering neon lights of the so-called 'Sin City' from ten miles away. She added that people in Las Vegas thought the girls odd for walking from where they were playing to their hotel – a distance of just a few hundred yards! Tired of explaining that they actually enjoy walking, the girls eventually capitulated and began to accept lifts from other members of the cast. 'They can't bear to see us walking' said Winnie.

The band then headed for Hollywood, and in April 1955 readers of the *Dagenham Post* back home must have done a double-take at a photo of the band lining up at the Hollywood Bowl nightclub wearing rhumba costumes, under the headline 'Pipers show a leg!' As we have seen, it was not uncommon for the girls to swell the chorus as well as giving their traditional performance.

Another unusual situation for the band occurred in May 1955 when they serenaded British boxer Don Cockell as he entered the ring for a world heavyweight championship fight against Rocky Marciano at San Francisco's Kezar Stadium. No doubt they were very disappointed to see Cockell get knocked out in the ninth round.

All told, the band spent an exciting 18 months in the USA and Canada, travelling 50,000 miles and helping to raise millions of dollars for children's hospitals by appearing at charity concerts. They eventually returned home at the end of March 1956. The girls linked arms as they got off the boat train at Waterloo Station, welcomed by two coachloads of relatives and friends. The band's return generated national newspaper publicity, and they also appeared on BBC TV's *In Town tonight*.

Drum Major Winnie Pile was soon in the news again. The American tour had been successful for her personally as well as professionally, for she had become engaged to Chester Stanley, manager of the Polack Brothers Circus, with which the girls had travelled. When the couple married in May 1956 at St Mary's Church in Ilford High Road, police had to be called in to control the

Winnie Pile (far right) and the band meet American singer Eddie Fisher in Hollywood *(the David Land Agency)*

crowds outside. Mr Land was best man, and the attendants were his children Lorraine and Brook, dressed in miniature pipers' uniforms. Winnie's band colleagues formed an archway of maces for the couple to walk through as they left the church.

And what of the band's activities at home while the American tour was taking place? In March 1955 huge crowds watched them lead the Chipperfield's Circus parade, complete with elephants, camels and other animals, from Romford Station along Rush Green Road to the Big Top site at Dagenham's Central Park. Bookings during summer that year included a trip to Holland during which they led a parade of Ford vehicles in Alkmaar. One unit undertook a six-week tour of Scotland, while another appeared in the David Whitfield show at Blackpool.

The main focus of events in 1955 was, of course, the band's own 25th birthday. A popular TV show of the day was *Ask Pickles* in which Wilfred Pickles offered viewers the chance to make their dreams come true (an early version, perhaps, of *Jim'll Fix It*, hosted by Jimmy Savile several decades later). Gladys Cross, one of the founding members of the band, had written to Mr Pickles asking him to contact Mr Graves, but the presenter decided to trace as many original band members as possible. Six of the twelve were found, and duly appeared on TV with Mr Graves. It was a poignant moment for them all, made even more so when the current band marched on and played *Auld Lang Syne*.

The Silver Jubilee anniversary itself in October was marked with a celebratory party at Dagenham County High School in Parsloes Avenue. Dagenham Borough Council presented the band with an illuminated address and two new drums, while Barton's came up trumps once more with a magnificent cake. Earlier in the week the band had marched through the City

The band's Silver Jubilee service in 1955: above, marching through the City of London
(*the David Land Agency);* below, arriving at St Paul's *(LBBD Archives at Valence House)*

of London to St Paul's Cathedral, where they gave a display on the forecourt
followed by a special service of thanksgiving and the re-consecration of their
banners and instruments.

New Year's Eve saw the band make its very first appearance on ITV, which had been broadcasting for only three months. In May 1956 they entertained the Wembley crowd at the FA Cup final between Birmingham City and Manchester City, which passed into legend as the match in which Manchester City's goalkeeper Bert Trautmann played on after suffering a broken neck in a collision.

A complete change of scene for the band came elsewhere that year, when they worked at Ealing Studios in the slapstick comedy *Who Done It?* which gave popular comedian Benny Hill his first major film role, playing a bumbling private detective.

Actress Belinda Lee goes undercover as a bass drummer with the band in *Who Done It? (the David Land Agency)*

In June 1957 came the publication of a hardback book *The Dagenham Girl Pipers* by Alfred H. Haynes, published by Faber at 7s 6d. The book's 191 pages provided a wonderfully detailed survey of the band's career across a quarter of a century of public performance. The dedication read 'At the special request of the directors this book is humbly dedicated to the parents of the Dagenham Girl Pipers in gratitude for their willing co-operation and many sacrifices'.

The author emphasised that the band's personnel was constantly changing, stating that over 500 girls had joined over the 27 years since its foundation. He listed the ranks on the promotion ladder as follows: joining as a Piper (equivalent to a private in the Army), a girl can progress is to Lance-Corporal, Corporal, Staff-Corporal, Sergeant, Staff-Sergeant and finally Pipe-Major.

He adds that 'The Drum-Major, whose spectacular whirling and tossing of the mace always arouses the admiration of the crowds, holds no seniority of rank. Strange to say, the efficient manipulation of the mace is an art which usually takes less time to acquire than piping; the showmanship and adroitness of outstanding Drum-Majors, however, are the result of many years of practical experience'.

Performing for the Queen Mother at Sandringham in the 1950s *(the David Land Agency)*

An audience of Dagenham children enjoy an impromptu show *(the David Land Agency)*

The book also detailed the cups awarded annually, in addition to the Graves Cup which had first been presented in 1948. They were: The Peggy Iris Cup, awarded on the results of competitive tests; the Lord Sempill Cup, given to the schoolgirl piper making most improvement over the year; the Pipe-Major's Cup, awarded to the year's best piper; the Lily Evans Dancing Cup; and the Colonel Bonner Cup, awarded to the outstanding drummer or Drum-Major of the year.

London's Oxford Street came to a standstill as the band marched to Selfridges for the book launch. The store devoted its main window to a display on the band.

In addition to this full history, several illustrated booklets were published in the 1950s to supplement the earlier *Piping through the War*. They included *Dagenham's Piping Ambassadors,* (issued soon after the accession of

Elizabeth II); *The Pipers from Dagenham* (commemorating the 25th anniversary); *The Dagenham Girl Pipers* and *Tartan and Lace,* both released in the late 1950s. They were sold by the junior girls at engagements for 2 shillings. The girls also made replica dolls which cost 25 shillings each.

During the summer of 1957 Mr Graves, now 76 and still living at Chestnut Wood near Sittingbourne, also turned his attention to writing. In his essay *Sixty Years a Preacher* he looked back at 'his pioneer Ministry in Dagenham; his lecture tours across the American continent and (perhaps most spectacular of all), his work as Founder of the famous Dagenham Girl Pipers...But finally he says to himself, 'My most precious meditation of all is that this is my Diamond Jubilee Year as a Preacher'.

Summer 1957 saw the band return to Scotland, appearing at the Edinburgh Festival, before making their way overseas on trips to Norway and Holland. In January of the following year, 1958, a milestone was reached with their first trip to a Communist country – Hungary. They stepped off the train in the capital, Budapest, at 11 o'clock in the evening to a crowd of press photographers, cameramen and reporters. Their concerts in the Grand Theatre were sell-outs, but the band was faced with two problems: freezing temperatures (the city was blanketed in four inches of snow), and the rule that

Preparing to leave for Hungary, 1958
(the David Land Agency)

currency could not be taken out of the country, which forced them to devise a bartering system to cover their day-to-day expenses.

Three months later the setting switched from communism to capitalism with a lightning tour of the USA alongside the Harlem Globetrotters basketball entertainment team, whose European agent was none other than Mr Land. The tight schedule involved travelling to twenty cities in nineteen days. Unfortunately the Atlantic liner was three days late in arriving at Halifax, Nova Scotia, so Mr Land hurriedly had to arrange air tickets so that the band could reach New York in time for the opening performances. Many of the girls had family and friends employed at the Ford factory in Dagenham, so a highlight of this tour must have been their visit to the Detroit headquarters, where they met the firm's President, Henry Ford II (grandson of the founder). They also had the luxury of staying in the Conrad Hilton Hotel in Chicago, then the largest in the world.

The American tour of 1958: ready to leave on the boat train; and returning with dollar bills
(the David Land Agency)

That same month, April 1958, textile manufacturer Courtaulds offered to supply the band with a large amount of material for new uniforms – in total 600 yards of black velveteen, 200 yards of tartan material, 200 yards of lining and 6 dozen pairs of hose. A delighted Mr Land commented that Courtaulds had been 'Fairy Godmothers helping us out of a Cinderella situation'. In return, the girls undertook promotion work on behalf of the firm at overseas trips such as the Brussels World Fair that August. The band flew to the World Fair in patriotic style by together with a fleet of specially painted red, white and blue Austin minibuses in the aircraft's hold, and were accompanied by the Mayor and Mayoress of Dagenham, Councillor and Mrs Matthew Eales.

Boarding the aircraft for Brussels, 1958; and finding their way about the city (*the David Land Agency*)

Meanwhile, six of their colleagues were on a thirteen-month tour of South Africa, Rhodesia and Tanganyika, visiting over 180 towns and cities. They returned in December 1958 on the liner *Stirling Castle*, just a day before the band's (postponed) 28th birthday party.

Leaving for South Africa, October 1957 (above left);
and the bass drummer gains a new leopard skin
(the David Land Agency)

July 1958 saw five band members joining *Ice-Capades*, an ice skating entertainment show touring the USA & Canada. They appeared in a Tribute to Scotland scene, and had to grin and bear it when the announcer introduced them as 'all the way from Dagenham, Scotland!' As usual, the girls received much media attention. In September they appeared on Ed Sullivan's *Toast of the Town* television programme, drawing 40 million viewers. The girls were thrilled to have long chat afterwards with a fellow guest, popular singer-songwriter and pianist Johnnie Ray, whose hits included *Just Walkin' in the*

Rain. In June 1959 two girls were travelling home on the liner *Queen Elizabeth* when they were snapped dancing the Highland Fling with the flamboyant pianist and entertainer, Liberace. When another two returned to Dagenham in May 1960 after two years with *Ice-Capades,* it was noticed that they spoke with American accents!

At the end of 1958 the band left for a four-week trip to Portugal, which would become the 41st country they had visited. It was noted that since 1952 there had been a band abroad all the time – a

A promotional postcard issued by the band in the 1950s *(Sheila Hatcher)*

remarkable feat of organization. New Year's Eve, as usual, saw band members performing at a variety of venues including the Chelsea Arts Ball at the Royal Albert Hall.

In August 1959 the band released an LP on the Top Rank label, and that summer also brought another tour of Scotland, including an appearance at the Edinburgh Festival. In September the band travelled to Spain, returning with the unusual souvenirs of three ears and a tail from a bullfight at Oviedo.

Towards the end of 1959 David Land was able to announce what he viewed as the best contract ever signed by the Pipers. Worth £25,000, it was a two-year engagement for a band of eight at the Paris Lido nightclub. A spectacular Highland scene was built around their act, with mountains, lakes and mist swirling around the stage. The club, home to the famous Bluebell Girls, could seat up to 3,000 people, and the audience often included celebrities such as Cary Grant, Sophia Loren and Gregory Peck. The girls were thrilled to see Elvis Presley there four nights running!

On stage with the Bluebell Girls at the Paris Lido *(Alma King)*

A typical Christmas show *(the David Land Agency)*

Chapter 5
The 1960s

The start of the new decade of the 1960s saw the band at the peak of its success. It had now visited 44 countries, and was seeking to recruit more girls with negotiations under way to send a massed band of about 100 to America for a coast-to-coast tour.

The band appealed to a wide range of audiences. At the beginning of the year, one unit was appearing with legendary clown Charlie Caroli in the pantomime *Goody Two Shoes* at the Empire Theatre, Leeds. And in April two girls were lucky enough to meet American teen idol Bobby Darin (whose hits included the timeless classics *Dream Lover* and *Beyond the Sea)* while performing in the TV show *Sunday Night at the London Palladium.*

A dressing-room photo of the band during the run of *Goody Two Shoes* (Sheila Hatcher)

Getting up close to pop idol Bobby Darin *(the David Land Agency)*

A tour of Norway and Sweden in summer 1960 was followed by the announcement that they had secured a £50,000 contract to play at the Tropicana nightclub in Las Vegas for 40 weeks, later extended to 14 months. Ten girls crossed the Atlantic on the liner *SS United States* in October, led by Staff Sergeant Selina Lee. They became accustomed to seeing Hollywood stars in the Tropicana audience, but when Elvis Presley was spotted one evening the excitement led to disaster for 17 year-old Bass Drummer Barbara Sawkins. Selina Lee wrote in a letter home that as the band waited in the wings 'Barbara nearly passed out when she saw Elvis. I had to tell her to pull herself together'. The girls marched on to the stage, but when Barbara took a swipe at her drum, the stick went right through the skin! David Land commented that 'I know Elvis has broken many hearts, but I'll bet this is the first time he has broken a drum skin!'

The temperature grew so hot the bagpipes had to be put in a freezer, and for some of the girls, romance was hotting up too. A front page headline in the *Dagenham Post* in July 1961 was 'Cupid takes his toll of pipers'. It reported that two of the ten performing in Las Vegas had married Americans, and a third had become engaged. David Land commented wearily that 'Cupid is my biggest problem. Although the girls sign non-marriage contracts when they go abroad, once Cupid appears on the scene they are worthless scraps of paper'. He said he had even considered taking out a Lloyd's insurance policy against girls getting married while on tour!

The *Dagenham Post* continued to give the band extensive coverage. In July 1960, for example, under the headline 'Higher and higher' and a photo of a mace seemingly heading for orbit, it told its readers that 17 year-old Christine Amor had broken a record by throwing the mace higher than any of her predecessors: 'twenty feet up, with a double somersault on the downward path'.

In August 1961 the band found themselves in the midst of a flashpoint in world events. A band of 10 girls were booked to appear on a radio and television show in West Berlin on 25 August. On 13 August the East Germans closed the border between East and West Berlin, and began demolishing entire streets of houses alongside the border. Construction of the notorious Berlin Wall was soon under way, sparking a major international crisis. When Mr Land applied to the Bow Street magistrates for the usual travel permits for the girls still under 18, he was given strict instructions. He had to accompany the band to Berlin, keep in close contact with the British Embassy, ensure that the girls did not go out unescorted, and take the first plane out of the city after the show finished.

The following month the band had a more comfortable overseas trip, this time to Naples where a squad of 25 pipers led the annual Piedigrotta carnival parade, watched by half a million people. The *Dagenham Post* reported that 'The Italians, it seems, have nothing like our pipers and the skirling music and colourful tartans have gone straight to their hearts. So much so that the City of Naples gave Pipe Major Peggy Iris (Peggio, to the Italians) a gold medal in tribute to all the pipers have done to foster international goodwill. A leading Rome Sunday newspaper devoted a whole page to a feature on the girls'. Foreign visits undertaken the following year, 1962, included a month-long engagement at the George Palest in Hanover, Germany.

Back in Britain, an amusing incident occurred in May 1962 when the band were playing at a Premium Bond draw. Since 1957 the numbers had been generated by ERNIE (Electronic Random Number Indicating Equipment). The normally reliable machine went haywire, and scientists ruled that the sound of the pipes had interfered with its sensitive electronic signals! David Land quipped that 'ERNIE must have fallen for the band's cute little numbers!' The girls had long been associated with National Savings. Sporting 'Buy Premium Savings Bonds' banners on their pipes, they had performed in November 1956 at the launch, when the Lord Mayor of London had bought the very first £1 Premium Bond.

Attempting to teach TV host Hughie Green to play the pipes
(the David Land Agency)

In the summer of 1962 the very sad news reached Dagenham that the band's founder, Joseph Waddington Graves, had died on 13 June at his home in Chestnut Wood, near Sittingbourne in Kent. He was 81 and had recently suffered a stroke. Without Mr Graves, of course, there would have been no Dagenham Girl Pipers. The original idea had been his, and he had pushed it forward by borrowing from his own insurance policies to train and equip the band.

Many former band members attended the funeral service for Mr Graves at Charing Crematorium. The pipers played a slow march as they led the cortege into the chapel, and sounded a lament at the close of the ceremony.

On Sunday 7 October 1962 a memorial service was held for Mr Graves at Osborne Hall, followed by the unveiling by Mrs Graves of an oak lectern, a gift from the band in memory of their founder and its dedication. An inscription around its base read: 'Presented by the Dagenham Girl Pipers in memory of their founder the Reverend Joseph Waddington Graves, who passed away 13 June 1962'.

Mr Graves (centre) is reunited with former band members in 1959
(Dagenham Girl Pipers Veterans Association)

DAGENHAM GIRL PIPERS

(REGD. OFFICE: 163, BROAD STREET, DAGENHAM, ESSEX)   FOUNDED BY REV. J. W. GRAVES, B.D.

DIRECTION:
Pipe Major PEGGY IRIS
DAVID LAND, M.I.P.R.
Pipe Major T. K. MARSHALL, M.V.O.

TELEPHONES:
GERrard 3224/5

TELEGRAMS:
Dagenham Girlpipers, London, W.1

CABLES:
GIRLPIPERS, DAGENHAM

THE INTERNATIONAL BAND

Address all communications to:
THE DIRECTOR,
DAGENHAM GIRL PIPERS,
118/120, WARDOUR STREET,
LONDON, W.1
GT. BRITAIN

A letterhead from the 1960s *(Iris Hamilton)*

On 25 July 1962 the band made their regular annual appearance at the Sandringham Estate Flower Show, forming a guard of honour for the Queen Mother and playing her favourite tunes such as *Over the Sea to Skye*. Peggy Iris, introduced to the Queen Mother, carried a new embroidered banner marking her 25 years as Pipe Major.

Such a glorious summer day was just a memory a few months later, when Britain fell into the grip of the coldest winter since the 18th century. In January 1963 ice floes stretched across the Thames at Tower Bridge, and the band were forced to cancel a performance in Cambridgeshire because their bagpipes were frozen solid. An astonished Peggy Iris commented that 'Even when I was playing to troops in Iceland during the war I never had a freeze-up!' Finally, in March 1963, the weather thawed and the country could get back to normal.

At this time the band had a contract to play at the opening of Fine Fare supermarkets. Their appearance at one in the north of England coincided with the making of the hit British film *Billy Liar*, directed by John Schlesinger and starring Tom Courtenay and Julie Christie. The band were seen parading out of a supermarket. In summer 1962 the band appeared at the London premiere of *The Music Man*, a film adaptation of a long-running Broadway musical comedy about the setting up of a boys' marching band.

At the *Music Man* premiere, 1962 *(Sheila Hatcher)*

During the summer of 1963 the band appeared for the first time at the annual family day of the large May & Baker chemical factory in Rainham Road South in Dagenham. They opened proceedings in the arena with a march and Highland dancing, and returned later for a finale of sword dancing and drum march-past.

That same summer, a band of eight toured Sweden with a circus for 6½ months. Their busy schedule began in the city of Malmo and involved much travelling and performances seven days a week. The beginning of 1964 saw another party off to join the circus, this time in Germany and Belgium, where some of the girls bravely agreed to ride on elephants! Piper Barbara Sawkins told the press that 'At first most of us were a bit

Meeting Roger Moore at a film premiere
(the David Land Agency)

frightened riding the elephants, but we soon got used to it. They were very gentle'.

By contrast, some of their colleagues were in the enviable position of performing with some of the biggest names in pop. Over Christmas and the New Year of 1963-4 one unit appeared in the pantomime *Babes in the Wood* with Gerry and the Pacemakers, the Liverpool band who had recently enjoyed three successive chart-topping singles including *I Like It* and *You'll Never Walk Alone*. In May 1964 a lucky group of girls travelled to Munich to take part in a TV show with the hugely popular Cliff Richard & the Shadows.

In September it was announced that a band of 8 had been booked to appear on Jimmy Logan's show in Glasgow, their first engagement in Scotland for three years. For their leader, 18 year-old Sandra Yard, it was a daunting challenge, as Peggy Iris admitted: 'It is a big occasion for Sandra. It's her first trip in charge of a band – and a trip to Scotland, of course, is an added thrill. The people there will really know what they are seeing, but happily any

Meeting Gerry and the Pacemakers in 1963 *(Sandra Jones)*

criticism is mostly constructive, and we have a great many friends across the border'.

Towards the end of October 1964 came another milestone, when the band returned to New York for the first time in ten years. The eight girls gave shows for other passengers as they crossed the Atlantic in a luxury liner. On one occasion the Duke and Duchess of Windsor were in the audience, and the Duke (formerly King Edward VIII) joined the band for an eightsome reel and invited them to dine at his table.

During their five-month stay in New York, the band performed at the Latin Quarter nightclub and appeared at the World's Fair. Their show at the Latin Quarter had elaborate sets, including real waterfalls. Their drums and

The girls at a photocall (left) before travelling to New York (the David Land Agency);
and (below) taking their bow on the Latin Quarter stage *(Sheila Hatcher)*

drumsticks were painted a fluorescent green, creating a spectacular effect when the lights went down. They returned on the *Queen Elizabeth* at the end of March 1965.

That spring, another unit left for on a tour of Switzerland which was planned to last for six months but was later extended to December. During the trip the girls visited over 60 towns and villages, travelling in circus wagons. Along the way they met people ranging from celebrities such as Yul Brynner, Mel Ferrer

and Charlie Chaplin, to an audience of prisoners at Zurich Jail. The same year saw the band visit Spain and also West Berlin, where they were performing with a circus but also had the opportunity of playing with a British Army band.

Back home, the band still regularly entertained the crowds at football matches. In April 1965 they played at their 14th FA Cup semi-final, but, as Mr Land joked, 'have never won the Cup!' On the 28th of that month they appeared at the memorable testimonial match for Sir Stanley Matthews. This was his last game for Stoke City after a career of more than 30 years, and the opposition was a Rest of the World team containing stars such as Lev Yashin, Alfredo di Stefano and Ferenc Puskas. The girls attended a celebratory ball afterwards.

A 1960s publicity shot
(the David Land Agency)

England went football mad the following year, 1966, when it hosted the World Cup. Barking and Dagenham had merged the previous year to form a single borough, and all its residents, including the Girl Pipers, were especially proud when England captain Bobby Moore received the winners' trophy from the Queen. Moore had been born and brought up in Barking, and his team-mate Martin Peters, the England manager Alf Ramsey and squad member Jimmy Greaves all hailed from Dagenham.

Later that same year, Peggy Iris flew to Singapore to face what was probably the biggest challenge of her entire career: setting up a girls' pipe band from scratch in time for them to take part in Singapore's National Day Parade in August 1967. Assisted at various times by Sheila Nobes, Irene Hamilton and Carole Cranfield, Peggy made several long stays in Singapore to set up the band and train an instructress. Despite the short period of training, the new band was praised on all sides at the National Day Parade.

In turn, two of the Singapore pipers spent several months training in Dagenham in Autumn 1967, and four years later the President of Singapore

The Singapore Girl Pipers march past the Presidential podium, 1967 *(Sheila Hatcher)*

himself arrived at Halbutt Street to watch band practice. The Singapore band have since had great success, including performing at the Edinburgh Tattoo.

Towards the end of 1966 two girls performed in nightclubs in Athens and Teheran, then in early 1967 the band turned its attention to two long-distance tours. The first was to Venezuela, a country they had not visited before. Before leaving the girls attended a reception at the Venezuelan consulate in London, and when they stepped off the 36-hour flight they found crowds lining the streets as they drove from the airport.

The band's second long-haul trip came in February 1967 when 25 girls left for a three-month tour of South Africa, sponsored by the Ford Motor Company of South Africa and South African Airways. They were the largest group to go overseas since 1939, when 25 had travelled to New York. The band

The 1967 South African tour:

Leaving from the Halbutt Street Drill Hall (above); and forming a guard of honour on their first day in South Africa (*Janet Stevens*)

Having a smashing time in a publicity shot in South Africa for Ford tractors *(Sheila Hatcher)*

flew to Johannesburg then travelled to Cape Town for the first show. They afterwards visited all corners of the country.

Back home, the band joined the rest of Britain in greeting the success of Dagenham girl Sandie Shaw, who triumphed in the Eurovision Song Contest in April 1967 with *Puppet on a String*. Born Sandra Goodrich, Sandie had grown up in Rainham Road North and on leaving Robert Clack School had worked for a time in an office at Fords.

At this time the band made several tours of the North of England club circuit, performing alongside chart-toppers such as Freddie and the Dreamers, Georgie Fame and the Blue Flames, Irish group the Bachelors and Billy J. Kramer. They were also making regular TV appearances, for example on the popular broadcasts of Billy Smart's Circus. In August 1966 they lined up with

The band on stage at the La Strada nightclub, South Shields *(Janet Stevens)*;
beer mats from Club Fiesta, Stockton-on-Tees *(Iris Hamilton)*

Hollywood star George Raft and Paul and Barry Ryan on the Rediffusion variety show *Hippodrome*, and in January 1968 could be seen on ITV's *Charlie Drake Show*, alongside the popular slapstick comedian whose catchphrase was 'Hello my darlings!'

Yet behind the scenes the band's financial position was causing anxiety. Travel and hotel costs were rising, and the new Selective Employment Tax also increased the wage bill. The number of full-time pipers, averaging wages of £2 10s a week, was allowed to dwindle to single figures, so that the majority were now part-timers, mostly schoolgirls. Yet even with these economies, income from bookings was failing to cover costs. In February 1968 the crisis broke with a shock announcement that the band would cease to operate in its present form. There was disbelief both locally and nationally at the prospect of the Dagenham Girl Pipers coming to an end.

Fifteen years previously, in 1952, Mr Land had suggested that Dagenham Council should adopt the band, backed by Alderman Brown, who declared 'There is no organisation in Dagenham more worthy of Council support than the Pipers'. The idea had not come to fruition then, but by 1968 everyone agreed the time had come for the local authority to act. Councillor James Beane called an emergency council meeting, telling the press: 'As far as I am concerned we are going to do all we possibly can to keep them going. It is these girls who have helped to put Dagenham on the map throughout the world. I am quite optimistic that something can be done. No-one wants to see the Girl Pipers die'.

The crisis as reported in the *Dagenham Post*, 7 February 1968

His fellow councillors agreed. The band would be re-constituted as a Voluntary Society under the auspices of Barking Council's Further Education Committee. The Mayor, Councillor Vic Rusha, would be the first band President, Mr Land was Chairman (and would continue to handle the bookings) and Peggy Iris the Administrator. Trustees included Councillor Ron Coster, who proved to be a strong supporter over the years (his daughter Janet was in the band).

The girls were called a meeting at Centre 64 in Vicarage Road. Peggy Iris told them 'From tonight we are going to start the new Girl Pipers...We are scrapping everything, and starting from scratch...This is not a full-time band, and everyone in it will be a volunteer, but, of course, you will all get expenses'.

A positive effect of the publicity was a surge in the number of applicants. A few weeks later Mr Land declared that 'We've had so many requests from young people wanting to join the Pipers that Peggy Iris and the other senior girls, who have been training them, just cannot cope with any more'.

Offers of engagements also flooded in, and the band found themselves busy every Saturday and a good many Sundays throughout the summer of 1968. In October that year they performed at the London premiere of the musical *Finian's Rainbow*, in the presence of the film's stars Tommy Steele and Fred Astaire. The band also continued to appear on the bill whenever the Harlem Globetrotters performed at Wembley Arena, and remained regulars at high-profile events such as the Spalding Flower Festival in Lincolnshire and the Battersea Park Easter Parade.

At the band's 38th birthday celebrations the usual annual awards were given, and the management also took the unprecedented step of awarding Graves Cup Special Mention certificates to 17 girls, without whose loyalty 'the Band would not be in existence today'. They were Joyce Reid, Carole Cranfield, Sheila Nobes, Sandra Bowling, Brenda Connelly, Janet Coster, Roberta Duhy, Iris Toleman, Rita

Even kilts followed the 1960s fashion for miniskirts! *(Iris Hamilton)*

Connolly, Anita Fenn, Sharon Fenn, Lily Field, Christine Fowl, Janette Hamilton, Carol Hardie, Lynn Keegan and Linda Webb.

Foreign engagements in 1969 included a fiesta and carnival in Madrid. One result of the new arrangements, however, was that the band now appeared more often at local events. July 1969 saw them in the Dagenham Town Show carnival parade for the first time (they had previously performed as an arena act, but had never marched in the parade to Central Park). As Mr Land explained, 'Now that the council have given us a home we are making a Thank You appearance at Dagenham'. Later that year came another first, when the Pipers led the Dagenham British Legion's Remembrance Day parade.

By the time of the band's 39th birthday party at Dagenham Park School, Peggy Iris was able to finish her speech on an optimistic note: 'We have created our own traditions, and traditions die hard'.

The band's annual awards for 1970 being presented by Councillor Vic Rusha. David Land appears in the back row, and Peggy Iris stands next to Mrs Rusha *(Linda Webb)*

Chapter 6
The 1970s - 1990s

At the time of the band's ruby anniversary in October 1970, Company Orders noted that 'At the present moment, our strength is in the region of 60 girls, and shows that interest in the band is still very much alive'. Speaking at the annual awards night, Peggy Iris said that 'It is almost three years since we became a society, and the training hours were cut. It was quite a problem keeping up our standard, but our girls have worked very hard, and they are a credit to Staff Sergeants Joyce Reid and Sheila Nobes'.

A 40th Anniversary Ball was held at Parsloes Manor School, at which Peggy was presented with a beautiful framed illuminated address, signed by members of the current band. Unfortunately a damper was put on the proceedings when a thief stole a five feet long mace from the car of Drum Major Irene Hunt. Weighing 9 pounds, with a silver chain wrapped around it and a thistle embossed on the head, it had originally been presented to Winnie Pile to commemorate the American tour of 1953-54.

In April 1972 bagpipe music received a huge boost when the hymn *Amazing Grace*, recorded by the pipes and drums and military band of the Royal Scots Dragoon Guards, spent five weeks at Number One in the charts and became the biggest-selling single of the year. For the band, the tune became an essential part of their repertoire when appearing at Wembley Arena with the Harlem Globetrotters. The Globetrotters shows could include improvised comedy. Janice Wells remembers one incident (pictured right). 'They came out during our part of the show wearing kilts, stole Irene Hunt's mace and my drum and brought the house down!'

(Janice Wells)

In 1973 Mr Land completed 25 years with the band, and to mark the occasion he was presented with a gold disc engraved with 'David Superstar Land'. This was a reference to him having 'discovered' Tim Rice and Andrew Lloyd Webber. Back in 1969, impressed by their short rock opera *Joseph and the Amazing Technicolour Dreamcoat*, he had offered them a contract to write a full-length work, which turned out to be the worldwide smash hit *Jesus Christ Superstar*. He even set up a room for them to work in, complete with piano, next to his own office in Wardour Street, Soho.

June 1973 saw the band appear in a multicultural event *East meets West* at Barking Assembly Hall, alongside traditional music and dancing from Pakistan, India and the West Indies. At this time the band also made regular trips to Witten, in Germany's Ruhr valley, the twin town of Barking and Dagenham. They also continued to make frequent appearances over Christmas and the New Year in circuses on the Continent, particularly in Italy and Spain. Christmas and New Year 1972-3, for example, was spent with the Circo Medrano in Florence.

Another highlight for the band that year was dressing in Edwardian costume to film scenes for the BBC series *Shoulder to Shoulder* at Holloway Prison. The

6-part series dramatized the story of the Suffragette movement, and starred Sian Phillips as Emmeline Pankhurst.

In 1975 the band held their 45th anniversary party at Dagenham Priory School. The prize-giving ceremony included a new cup, awarded to the best drummer, named after staff sergeant Joyce Reid who had given 25 years' service to the band.

In March 1976 band members were shocked to hear of the theft of their ceremonial swords, all vintage claymores dating from before 1914. Peggy Iris declared that 'The girls are very upset as they can't do the usual sword dance in their act.' Replacements were soon offered, though, by firms including razor manufacturer Wilkinson Sword. By the time the stolen swords were recovered in an attic, Mr Land was able to declare 'We have enough swords to start an uprising!'

Prizewinners at the 1974 birthday awards ceremony *(Janice Wells)*

Peggy Iris receiving her BEM. Mr Land is on the left *(Sheila Hatcher)*

When the Queen's Birthday Honours list was announced in June 1976, there was cause for more celebration at the news that Pipe Major Peggy Iris had been awarded the British Empire Medal. Peggy told the *Barking Advertiser* that 'Receiving the BEM was a great surprise to me, but I only got the honour because I front the band'. She added 'For as long as I am capable, I will carry on with the band. It is not work to me, it is a pleasure. My whole life is wrapped up in it and I enjoy every minute'.

Peggy received the award at the in London's County Hall on the South Bank from the Lord Lieutenant of Essex. Peggy had a high profile on the road, too, as her car bore the number plate DGP2. She was once waiting at traffic lights when a man knocked on the window wanting to buy the plate!

In October 1976, ten girls flew to Oman for a trip which including performing at the Gulf Hotel before Sultan Qaboos Bin Said. The *Barking Advertiser* couldn't resist printing the story below a punning headline typical of the 1970s: 'Blow me – they're sheiking all over!'

The special guest at the Pipers' 47th anniversary party at Dagenham Priory school, was Tim Rice who, like the band, was managed by David Land. He presented the citations and cups to the year's outstanding performers.

The band appeared alongside another showbiz great, Max Bygraves, at the opening of the Coral Bingo and Social Club in Green Lane, Dagenham in July 1978. Max, as we have seen, had lived in Dagenham and Rush Green for several years after the war, and had regularly sung at local venues such as the Merry Fiddlers pub at Beacontree Heath.

At a speedway meeting in the late 1970s *(the David Land Agency)*

The band had received many tributes in their time, but June 1980 saw something completely different, in the shape of a pub in Dagenham named the Pipers! It stood at the junction of Gale Street and Woodward Road, near Becontree Station. Formerly the Fanshawe Tavern, it underwent a £160,000 refurbishment before being re-launched as the Pipers in June 1980. The idea was not new – back in 1957 a brewery wanted to call a new pub the Girl Piper, but Mr Land objected because they had not asked permission, and the idea was eventually dropped. As for the Pipers pub, it welcomed drinkers for over two decades before an announcement at the end of 2002 that it was to be demolished and replaced by flats.

The band's stand-out event in 1980, of course, was its 50th anniversary, culminating in a party and concert on 4 October at Barking Assembly Hall attended by many former band members, some of whom had travelled from all over Britain and abroad. The Mayor and other local dignitaries attended, but the undoubted guests of honour were Mrs May Graves and her daughter Brenda. Mrs Graves was delighted to see so many familiar faces, but was by then very frail, and would pass away four years later aged 82.

Ticket for the 50th
anniversary ball
(Sheila Hatcher)

At the party Peggy Iris was presented with a carriage clock and flowers. She told *the Times* that 'We might not win any prizes at a pibroch contest on the Isle of Skye, but we've tried to broaden the appeal of pipe music'. As the 1980s progressed, Peggy gradually lessened her involvement with the band. She finally retired in 1987 after 57 years of service, and was succeeded as Pipe Major by Sheila Hatcher (formerly Sheila Nobes).

In 1981 the band performed on ITV's *An Audience with Dudley Moore*. They were chosen because Moore also hailed from Dagenham, and attended Dagenham County High School. He had achieved fame as a comedian, musician and had become an unlikely Hollywood heart-throb in the movie *10*. He had recently starred in *Arthur*, with Liza Minnelli and John Gielgud, and in the *Audience with...* show he duetted with singer-songwriter Christopher Cross on the movie's theme song *The Best that You Can Do*.

A group shot from the 1980s *(the David Land Agency)*

Lily Field (left) and Sheila Hatcher perform at London City Airport
(the David Land Agency)

The 1980s also saw the band supporting Rod Stewart at his Wembley Arena concerts. This was appropriate because although Rod's father was Scottish, he himself is Sassenach like the Girl Pipers – born in North London and currently living in Essex! The band's television appearances during that time included shows with Roy Castle, Des O'Connor and Kenny Everett.

Moving forward into the next decade, the year 1991 brought both heartbreak and triumph for the band. In August they were shocked by a break-in at their store at Centre 64 in Vicarage Road. Medals and trophies gathered over the years were stolen, and the intruders had wrought much wanton damage– drum skins were broken, uniforms pulled apart and bagpipes smashed.

Ironically, the collection was due to be transferred to new premises at Dagenham Priory School just a few days later. An appalled Sheila Hatcher told the *Dagenham Post* 'The place is an absolute wreck. They destroyed almost everything. What did they get out of it? Now all we have left is the equipment we were using at a small show over the weekend'.

The Pipers now faced the real prospect of having to disband. Happily, though, their supporters rallied round with offers of cash and equipment. Thanks to this assistance and their own hard work, the band were able to stage a dramatic comeback in November at one of the biggest arenas of all - the Royal Variety Performance at London's Victoria Palace Theatre. It was the first time since 1963 that the band had taken part, and they found themselves in a surreal sketch alongside Eric Idle of the Monty Python team, Sumo wrestlers and high-kicking Tiller Girls! Afterwards Prince Philip chatted to the Pipers and told them how much he and the Queen had enjoyed the show.

The end of 1995 saw the band in mourning when their manager David Land died suddenly after a heart attack on Christmas Eve, aged 77. As we have seen, Mr Land's astonishing career had taken him from a small shop in Broad Street to the pinnacle of show business as the mentor of Tim Rice and Andrew Lloyd Webber. Yet, as he told the *Daily Telegraph*: 'It's a standing gag in this

Leading a Remembrance Day parade in Church Street, Dagenham, in the 1990s
(the David Land Agency)

business, but if you ring up to discuss a production of *Jesus Christ Superstar* you don't get put through to me. But say you're getting married in Barking, and need a couple of pipers, I'm immediately on the phone!'

Sir Tim Rice paid this tribute: 'His achievements in many different fields of show business were outstanding, but above all he will be remembered and missed as a supremely warm and funny man'. Mr Land was heard to say that he planned to start a business one day called Hope and Glory, so that when he answered the phone he could say 'Land – of Hope and Glory!'

Mr Land's funeral took place on Boxing Day 1995 at Willesden Synagogue. Some years previously, he had bought Brighton's Theatre Royal, saving it from the threat of closure, and it was here that a memorial concert was held for him three months later. The band performed at the occasion, as did Vera Lynn, who had also been managed by Mr Land. Reassuringly, the David Land Agency continue to handle the band's bookings.

In April 1997 the band heard that they would be given the honour of carrying the colours of the Borough of Barking & Dagenham for the coming year, a task they had last carried out in 1980-1981. They collected the colours at the Dagenham Town Show in July.

In May 1997 the band headed the Barking Carnival Festival, a walking procession from Barking Park to the Abbey Green. They marched alongside the Mayor, Councillor

Wood carving of a Dagenham Girl Piper
(Vic Pountney)

The band pose with a clown while appearing at a circus in Bilbao in 1997 *(Iris Hamilton)*

John Wainwright, and his wife Yvonne, who as Yvonne Smith had been a Dagenham Girl Piper in the 1960s. They were joined by stilt-walkers, street entertainers and local community groups.

The band's engagements on the Continent in the late 1990s included several carnivals in France, such as one in Lille in which the parade lasted five hours! In August 1997 they travelled to Bilbao in Spain to appear with the circus Gran Circo Mundial. Not only did they present their act in the circus ring for three performances a day, but they were also called upon to parade between the showground and the town to publicize the event.

TV appearances during this period included *Talking Telephone Numbers*, hosted by Phillip Schofield, and the *Gloria Hunniford Show*.

As the 1990s drew to a close, everyone's thoughts turned towards the long-heralded Millennium reunion.

PIPERS' MAJOR EVENT

THE original Dagenham Girl Pipers from 1930 were in fine form again when they teamed up for the homecoming of the group's first ever pipe major, Edith Turnbull.

Edith, 75 started a new life in America 50 years ago when she married a sergeant in the US army. But she was delighted to fly back last week for a mini dress rehearsal of a date marked in every Dagenham Girl Piper's diary.

Group founder Joseph Waddington-Graves signed an agreement with his pipers in 1936 that every girl, old and new, would meet on the steps of the Town Hall at noon on January 1, 2000.

Mrs Ivy Riley, who hosted the gathering said: "We obviously had a lot to talk about after all these years."

A *Dagenham Leader* report of 14 September 1994 detailing
the first meeting to plan the Millennium reunion
(Dagenham Girl Pipers Veterans' Association)

Chapter 7

The 21st century

As we have seen, 53 girls signed a pledge on 21 October 1938 to meet at noon on 1 January 2000 on the steps of the Civic Centre. Over the years many former members of the band had kept in touch. In October 1959, for example, Grace Richards had arranged for a party of 18 to visit Mr and Mrs Graves at their home in Kent. In Spring 1974 the first official reunion was held at Corringham in Essex. Over 150 veterans attended, including three of the 12 original members, Peggy Iris, Gladys Cooper and Gladys Cross. In 1977 another reunion, plus an exhibition of band memorabilia, was staged at Campion School in Hornchurch and drew an attendance of 250.

Plans for the Millennium event got under way in summer 1994, spurred on by a rare visit to England by Edith Turnbull, the band's first home-grown Pipe Major. The *Barking & Dagenham Post* headlined her arrival with 'Pied Piper of Brooklyn comes home'. Edith told the paper 'It's great to be back in Dagenham. For many years I lived in Brooklyn, close to the bridge, but never forgot those early days with the band'.

Initial discussions about the reunion were held at the home of Ivy Richards, attended by the three Turnbull sisters Edith, Annie and Mary, plus ten other band veterans. A further get-together at Marks Gate Hall in July 1994 attracted 29 girls.

In April 1998, with less than two years to go before the big day, the Dagenham Girl Pipers Veterans' Association was formed. Grace Richards

Below: the appeal to trace the signatories from 1938 is launched in 1998
(Dagenham Girl Pipers Veterans' Association)

(Mrs Simmonds) was appointed Secretary, and the Chairman was Graham Jardine, whose mother Lily Vale and several aunts had been in the band.

Over the years many former band members had moved away, some to other countries, so the Association's most pressing task was to trace as many as possible of the girls who had signed the pledge. In June 1998 an appeal was launched at the Ford Heritage Centre in Dagenham and widely publicized in the press. Eventually more than 40 of the original 53 were tracked down, some living in the USA or Canada.

Millennium Day itself was celebrated in different ways the length and breadth of Britain, but as noon approached the eyes of the media turned towards the Civic Centre in Dagenham. A BBC camera crew and radio reporters arrived, joined by crowds of onlookers. The stars of the show then made their way to the steps – twenty women, some in their eighties, who had signed the pledge almost 62 years before. Two had been part of the first practice session of 4 October 1930: Doris Patterson and Peggy Iris.

The reunion was broadcast live on BBC1, with millions watching as the veterans repeated the words of the pledge before being interviewed by reporter Richard Lindley. Over 80 other former band members also attended, and the current band paraded on the Civic Centre forecourt. The veterans then attended a service at Osborne Hall before going on to a celebratory party at the headquarters of the Dagenham branch of the Royal British Legion in Rectory Road.

The *Dagenham Post* summed up the event. 'Few Millennium celebrations were as poignant, or as meaningful. The years just fell away as friends were reunited on such a special day'. Grace Richards said 'It's been absolutely fantastic. Crowds of people were here to see the reunion, and it was very

The Veterans are joined by the current band on the Civic Centre steps, January 1st 2000
(Dagenham Girl Pipers Veterans' Association)

Peggy Iris speaking at the Osborne Hall service *(Dagenham Girl Pipers Veterans' Association)*

moving. I can't find words to describe how it felt to be together again. It has taken two years to organize, and has been so worthwhile'.

Peggy Iris was equally delighted. 'It's been a wonderful reunion, I was a teenager when we signed the pledge and I remember thinking we would never live until the year 2000. There were some girls I hadn't seen since the war. But I recognized their faces, even if I couldn't remember everyone's name straight away'. Sadly, Edith Turnbull was forced to remain in the USA due to ill-health. Her granddaughter Kristine Kirby-Webster attended in her place, however, having promised to record every detail of the event. Kristine also brought Edith's pipes and a plaque, which she presented to the current Pipe Major, Sheila Hatcher.

The year 2000 was also the band's 70th birthday. The anniversary proper was celebrated in October with an exhibition at Dagenham's Valence House Museum and a party at Dukes Hall in Hornchurch. The role of Chairman of the Veterans's Association was now held by Ivy Richards (Mrs Riley), and its members were kept in touch by means of a newsletter, *Piper'sing Times*.

The year 2001 began with the band leading the Barking & Dagenham Council float in the New Year's Day Parade through the streets of London. The float celebrated Barking's fishing heritage and local personalities such as Captain James Cook, who was married at St Margaret's Church. The float won sixth prize and £500 towards the Mayor's Beeline 2000 appeal, supporting five local charities. Early in February the band attended a celebratory reception at Eastbury House in Barking.

Later that month, band members past and present gathered at the Civic Centre once again. This time the occasion was the unveiling of a brass plaque, to be placed in the Mayor's Parlour, in memory of their founder Joseph Waddington Graves. The current band performed music for the occasion as the Mayor, Mr Pat Manley, greeted the guests. Mr Manley, a long-term supporter of the band, had been instrumental in obtaining permission for the plaque to be installed, and would later become President of the Veterans' Association.

The inscription on the plaque read: 'He made his dream come true and in doing so gave to so many young girls from Dagenham opportunities, music and wider horizons that would otherwise have been out of their reach. Now, 70 years on, we past and present pipers who profited by his endeavours remember him and give thanks for his time with us'.

The guests included around 50 girls who had been in the band in Mr Graves's day. Grace Richards told the press that 'We, as youngsters, marched the streets of Dagenham and carried the Borough's name around the world. The pipers have done thousands of miles over the 70 years on behalf of the Borough. It's only right and proper the Pipers' founder is remembered and given a place of honour in Dagenham'.

As the year 2001 drew to a close, news arrived from America of the death of Edith Turnbull at the age of 82. As we have seen, at only 17 she had made history by becoming the world's first female and first non-Scottish Pipe Major. A memorial service was held for Edith early in 2002 at Dagenham Parish Church. A tribute was read from her granddaughter: 'Despite attaining worldwide acclaim with the Girl Pipers, she always remained a girl from Dagenham - quiet and unassuming'. Peggy Iris played Edith's favourite tune *Amazing Grace*, and the current band piped a Lament at the beginning and end of the service.

May 2002 saw a happier occasion for the band when Queen Elizabeth II visited Eastbury House as part of her Golden Jubilee tour of Britain. The Pipers played and marched on the lawn in front of the house entertaining the waiting crowd before the Queen's arrival, and were later introduced to her.

Waiting for the Queen to arrive at Eastbury House, May 2002 *(Gordon Dickerson/Ken & Richard Chapman collection)*

Two months later the band prepared to lead the Golden Jubilee Dagenham Town Show parade from Old Dagenham Park to Central Park. Sergeant Tracy Deller told the *Barking & Dagenham Post:* 'The younger girls especially are getting excited about it. We normally start the little ones off in the Carnivals so they become used to people. But it's hard work organising and actually marching the route – it's a long carnival to walk, about 3 miles and the drums are heavy!'

The summer of the following year, 2003, BBC Radio 4 broadcast a history of the band entitled *Girls with Skirls*, researched and presented by Stewart Henderson for Whistledown Productions. In October 2003 the band performed at local undertaker West & Coe's 100th anniversary dinner and cabaret. The event took place in a huge marquee at Dagenham's Central Park, and other performers included comedian Ronnie Corbett and actress Linda Robson.

In November the band took their usual place at the head of the annual Remembrance Parade of the Dagenham branch of the Royal British Legion. The route began at the Legion's headquarters in Rectory Road and ended with

At Valence House for the 60th anniversary of VE Day, 2005 *(Barking & Dagenham Post)*

a service at Dagenham Parish Church in the presence of the Mayor and Dagenham's MP Jon Cruddas. The band also led similar processions marking the 60th anniversaries of D-Day in 2004 and VE Day in 2005, and attended Valence House Museum's VE Day commemoration event in May 2005.

The year 2005, of course, marked the band's 75th anniversary. The Veterans' Association was awarded a well-deserved Lottery-funded Home Front Recall grant in recognition of the band's role during World War Two. It staged a glittering reunion at the Dagenham & Redbridge Football Club in Victoria Road, Dagenham. During the evening Peggy Iris, then 86, played a solo and was then joined by the current band. The Association also commissioned a memorial drum for the occasion, on which were written the names of deceased members. Valence House Museum began an oral history project the same year, recording memories of some of the veterans.

The band continued to be seen regularly on television in the new century, in programmes including ITV1's *Off the Beaten Track* and the *Jonathan Ross Show* on the BBC. In January 2007 they were guests of Channel 4's popular chat show host Paul O'Grady, who introduced them as 'the legendary

Leading the Dagenham British Legion Remembrance Day parade in 2007
(Barking & Dagenham Post)

Dagenham Girl Pipers.' Hilarious scenes ensued as the girls attempted to teach the basics of drumming and Highland dancing to Paul and their fellow-guests Martin Kemp (of Spandau Ballet) and *Coronation Street* actress Gaynor Faye. In January 2008 the band appeared on the Channel 4 Political Awards show, presenting Dagenham MP Jon Cruddas with an award for the best campaigning politician.

We now reach October 2010, exactly 80 years since the band's very first practice session on 4 October 1930. The Dagenham Girl Pipers Veterans' Association held a party at Dagenham & Redbridge Football Club at which generations of girls met once more and reminisced, accompanied by music from the current band.

The band's 80th birthday cake, with a photograph of Mr Graves, the founder
(author's collection)

In summer 2010 Dagenham's Valence House Museum reopened after a two-year refurbishment. Visitors could admire a new permanent display devoted to the Dagenham Girl Pipers, including the uniform worn by Peggy Iris as Pipe Major. The museum also launched a temporary exhibition on the band in October 2010, the centrepiece being a large portrait of Peggy painted for the 25th anniversary in 1955.

Looking back over the band's extraordinary 80-year story, which has taken it from small beginnings as a Sunday school band to worldwide fame, we can echo the words spoken in 1970 by the late Councillor Vic Rusha, the band's first President:

'Rock groups come and go, but the Pipers go on forever'.

The band performing at Valence House in October 2010 *(author's collection)*

Bass drummer Ivy Richards in the 1940s
(Dagenham Girl Pipers Veterans' Association)

Chapter 8
Some memories

Doris Patterson (in the band 1930-39)

'*I* *was one of the original 12 who formed the band to prove we could play as well as the boys. It took us 18 long months and a lot of hard work before we could play in public. One of the most moving things we did was to play a lament in Ypres in 1933, remembering the war dead. The outbreak of war ended my career with the band but the discipline it imposed was very good for me. I supported myself for the rest of my life'.* ©The Daily Mail 1999

Mary Turnbull (in the band 1931-47)

'*I* *had been working in an office before I persuaded Mr Graves to let me join the band like my sister Edith. It was so exciting, even though we were practising twice a day and on Saturday mornings. My husband started courting me when he saw me with the Pipers, but I wanted to travel before I settled down – I went to Holland, Belgium and France'.* ©The Daily Mail 1999

Joan James (in the band 1933-45)

'*I* *was an 11 year-old schoolgirl from Dagenham who thought joining the Pipers might occupy my time. I didn't realise then what a chance I was being given. My favourite time was the two years we spent at the London Palladium in the show* Happy and Glorious *with stars such as Tommy Trinder. The most exciting night was when we went to Windsor Castle the day before the Armistice was declared to perform before the Royal Family. The then Princess Elizabeth thanked us personally...The most important thing that the Pipers taught me is that life is what you make of it'.* ©The Daily Mail 1999

Joan Edwards (in the band 1934-46)

'*Once we came face to face with Hitler himself, just before the war, when he attended one of our concerts in Berlin. We didn't think much of him, in fact we took no notice of him because we thought he was just another VIP. We had no inkling of what was about to happen. We were told he said "I wish I had a band like that". I had to go part-time with the Pipers during the war because I was called up for war work. But I was allowed to perform at Windsor Castle for George VI where I met my heroes – Arthur Askey, Vera Lynn and the Crazy Gang. After I got married I had to give up, and missed it very much*'.
©The Daily Mail 1999

Lily Vale (in the band 1934-41)

'*I was 11 years old when I joined…It was something different from Brownies and Girl Guides. First band practice was a comforting introduction under the gentle wing of Senior Sergeant Mary Turnbull. First 12 months on a practice chanter to learn the scales and tunes was good preparation to master the skill of playing the bagpipes, and I very soon accomplished it. My first tunes were* Blue Bonnet, Scotland the Brave *and* Bonnie Dundee. *My first public performances were street parades and garden fetes in and around Dagenham, always lots of people. I specialised in piping, and eventually piped for the dancing with Edith Turnbull.*

We met many celebrities and Royalty on that first trip the band made to America in 1939, such famous people came to see us perform. I feel so humble now to think we were so young, and so well chaperoned, strict discipline and all our welfare and needs taken care of.

I left the band to take up nursing as my war effort, but continue to still have strong emotions for pipes and drums. Am now 86 years, and have lots of stories to tell my grandchildren'.   ©Lily Vale 2010

Margaret Fraser (in the band 1935-45)

'*I loved my ten years with the Pipers but the highlight was the three years in Africa during the war performing for the troops in the El Alamein campaign. I did a duet with another Piper, Peggy Iris. We travelled in all sorts of strange vehicles including Army trucks and flying boats. I was only 18, so it didn't seem scary, except for the insects. We had quinine every day but I still fell ill with malaria. There I was, seeing Tutankhamun's tomb and the Pyramids, but we always knew our priority was entertaining the boys, and I was awarded the Africa Star'.* ©The Daily Mail 1999

Pat Arnold (in the band 1935-45)

'*My favourite bit was the uniforms – putting on the kilt, tartan socks, velvet jackets and tam-o'-shanters. We were meant to be good but by friend in the band, Ivy Spooner, was the saucy one – she used to twirl the chorus boys into the curtains! My dancing came to an end after I fell down a lift shaft on tour. When we made the Pledge we couldn't believe we'd meet up again – we thought we'd be so old!'* ©The Daily Mail 1999

Jean Harrison (in the band 1936-50)

'*My family were ever so proud of me because we were too poor even to afford a holiday and, suddenly, there I was travelling the world. Of course, it was very strict. We weren't meant to wear nail varnish or have boyfriends, but I went out with Eric Morley [organiser of Miss World] when he was publicity agent for Mecca Dance Halls. I became engaged for a time to a German Baron, Alexander von Scotti, a former prisoner of war whom I met on tour. I will always remember those wonderful years'.* ©The Daily Mail 1999

Margaret Williams (in the band 1936-50)

'*I was just an ordinary girl from an ordinary family, given this amazing chance to see the world. Even the day war was declared, I was thousands of miles away from home in a Canadian church. We all burst into tears because we didn't know what it would mean. I was called up to do war work in Fords. I was very unhappy, and the Rev. Graves came and rescued me, telling the Ministry: "This girl will be far more useful entertaining the troops can working here!" The Ministry agreed, and so I spent the war in the Middle East. I stayed in Rommel's former house. I think the main effect the Pipers had on me was that I acquired a great love for travel, which has stayed with me all my life*'.
©The Daily Mail 1999

Joyce Reeland (in the band 1936-50)

'*The Rev. Joseph Graves's house was at the bottom of our garden, and when he found out I played the violin and piano he asked me to help out with the music. It was marvellous, the most exciting thing that has ever happened to me. Then the war started and I was forced to drive ambulances, so I dashed to engagements when I wasn't on shift. As soon as the war was over I rejoined full-time and went to India and Ceylon. Then my mother became ill with Parkinson's Disease and I had to devote my life to her. The Pipers taught you your duty and I was jolly glad I did look after her but, oh, I did miss the fun of the band!*'
©The Daily Mail 1999

Margaret ('Mickey') Child (in the band 1936-50)

'*Each Wednesday evening the noticeboard would be scanned to see who was on what engagement for the following weekend. I was overwhelmed when I saw that I was to go on my first engagement the following Saturday. It was a British Legion fete. My balloon soon burst when I discovered I was down, not to play the bagpipes or the drums, but to sell postcards of the band. This rather dented my enthusiasm for a while, but, as it was pointed out to me, I was one of the very, very junior girls, and everybody had to start from the bottom! Fortunately the weather was good and there was a large crowd, and I managed to dispose of quite a few postcards...I did this on one or two engagements, but soon realised even at my young age, the more I sold the longer I would be on 'postcard duty!' So I don't think I tried too hard, and my salesmanship dropped off...'*

©Mickey Child 2010, from her book *One of a kind: notes on memoirs of a Pied Piper*

Lilian Hubbard (in the band 1936-40)

'*I rushed round to Mr Graves on my 11th birthday begging to join. We had some amazing experiences. On the 1939 German tour, Stormtroopers came into the hotel to check we were enforcing the curfew. We were terrified and got out of the country quickly. When the band temporarily disbanded at the start of the war my family moved to Hampshire so I never went back. I found it heartbreaking. My few years with them inspired me always to make the best of life. I still teach dancing today'.* ©The Daily Mail 1999

Annie Turnbull (in the band 1937-51)

'*From the age of four, I was desperate to join my sisters. Because I joined later when war was on the horizon I didn't get to go to America or many of the foreign places. When war broke out I went to work at Fords but I did carry on with the band as well. I left in 1951 because I was getting married. I had never had any musical ambitions but after my experience in the Pipers I made sure my three daughters all played instruments, and I'll make sure my grandchildren do the same'.* ©The Daily Mail 1999

Grace Richards (in the band 1937-43)

'*I joined the band at the age of 11. My father had heard of the band before our family moved to Dagenham, and soon after we arrived he went to Mr Graves asking if I could join. The first tune I learned to play on the pipes was* Lord Lovat's lament. *My first band engagement was at the Ostend Casino nightclub. Because I was under 16 I had to go with Mr Graves to Bow Street Police Station in London to get permission to travel. Other performers at the nightclub included Maurice Chevalier and Josephine Baker.*

In 1938-9 we were performing at the Kilburn State Gaumont Theatre on the variety bill between the films. It was showing Angels with Dirty Faces, *which we saw around 35 times! It was a big theatre. As we marched to our places on the stage, the pipers had to come through the back of the stage while the drummers went underneath and were brought up on a moving stage. I was one of two tenor drummers, at the back. The moving stage came up slowly, then just stopped before I was off it. The audience could just about see my arms and the drumsticks twirling above the stage. I was afraid it would jerk up and catapult me out!*

During World War Two I became a Land Girl. I stayed at Mr Graves's cottage at Great Sampford while working on a farm nearby. Also during the war, I went with the band to Denham Studios to make a film about women at war, which also included Ivy Benson's band.

In 1943 I became unwell and was unable to continue piping. I then became Personal Assistant to Mr Graves in his London office at 123 Craven Street, Charing Cross. In 1959 I organized the first reunion of band veterans. I wrote to the other girls asking them to meet at Dagenham Heathway Station for a "mystery trip". We went to Deal in Kent to see Mr and Mrs Graves and Brenda, and had a lovely day. I'm now Secretary of the Veterans' Association, and have been involved in organizing several reunions, including the Millennium Day reunion'. ©Grace Richards 2010

Shirley Duffin (in the band 1941-51)

'*I was a little girl of 11 years of age in Sunday School at Osborne Hall Congregational Church...The Reverend Graves was a regular visitor to our church, and asked if anyone would like to apply... When I left school, during the war, I was engaged full-time, and enjoyed some very exciting engagements. Also I joined the No. 2 Touring Band and worked for ENSA and then the Combined Services Entertainment Unit.*

The band obtained a long-term contract to perform with Cirque Amar in France in 1947...I was selected to go, but being just under the age of 18 had to have not only my parents' permission, but also had to go to Bow Street Magistrates' Court for permission to work overseas, which was granted provided we had a chaperone. Fortunately at that time one of the girls, Margaret Baxter, had recently married, so her husband came along as manager/chaperone. We left England in January 1947. The snow was so deep that I remember my father having to dig a path from our house to the coach.

Next stop Paris, and then the midnight train to Marseilles, where we were met at the station by clowns, jugglers, animals and the management. We all paraded through the town, with pipes playing and drums beating. The whole circus moved by train (its own train) – the Big Top, all the animals, the artists, who were multi-national, and all the other staff, which included some German prisoners of war who were awaiting repatriation to Germany.

The train was divided up into main living accommodation. We had three sections: the married couple had one, eight of us girls had another, and the third was the cookhouse. In our section we had bunk beds...

. The next ten months we travelled all over France, but at that time France was going through a period of political and social unrest, caused mainly by the Communist party, and on a number of occasions they threatened to blow up the train. Often they blew up letter boxes, and the mail wasn't getting through to our families back in England.

We arrived back in Marseilles and were told the circus was going to North Africa to join up with the Amar Brothers Circus... All the animals were shipped off, and a couple of days later the artists and other staff left by boat. We did ask why we were going separately, but didn't get a convincing or straight answer, so became a little concerned. However, the following day, by chance the Manager, myself and another member saw Amar (the owner) take a revolver from a drawer in his caravan and slip it in his pocket.

We found the address of the British Consul and went to see him. When we gave him the facts he told us "You must leave immediately without drawing attention to yourselves". He arranged for us to board a train to Paris, with two security men in the background. On arriving at Gare du Nord Station in Paris we were accompanied by two new security men from the British Embassy, who travelled with us to Calais, then put us on a ferry to England. We all arrived home with very little, as we had to leave all our belongings behind in the caravan. Eventually our instruments were recovered, but not our personal things'.
©Shirley Duffin 2010

Jean Vale (in the band 1942-49)

'*My two sisters, Kathleen and Lilian Vale, joined the band in the Thirties and I was always taken to see them off on band engagements, so I wanted to join the band from a very young age...*

We learned on a practice chanter for many months before going on to bagpipes. During that time we learned the fingering and to read music. This was very helpful when it came to mastering the bagpipes, which was a matter of learning the control of air blown into the pipebag, activating the drone reeds and chanter reed. It took time but we all managed it.

Apart from parades and outdoor events, my first full time work with the band began in 1944 when I was fifteen and it was on ENSA (Entertainment National Service Association). Catterick Camp actually had the accommodation for us on the camp, and it was there we were based when the war ended...There was a formal announcement of the Victory in Europe after the show that night.

In 1946 Mr. Graves sent me to the London Palladium where band members had been in a show called Happy and Glorious *for two years...It ended in the spring of 1946 and a band of us were then leaving for a tour of Sweden, which lasted all summer... I went as Drum Major, which was new to me, having always been a piper. Our first parade in Sweden was at Malmo. It was a huge 88th birthday parade for their King Gustav. It was a very big event for my first band engagement as a Drum Major.*

The Royal Command Performance in 1947 certainly was very exciting...At the party after the show we surrounded Laurel and Hardy and they were so friendly and had photos taken with some of the girls'.   ©Jean Vale 2010

Ivy Richards (in the band 1942-49)

'*I joined the band after coming back to Dagenham after being evacuated early in the war. I was fast-tracked into the band because my older sister Grace was ill, and as it was wartime Mr Graves needed to take on young recruits to replace some of the older girls away on war work. We were taught the basics of the chanter by Pat Arnold, who was convalescing after breaking her back falling down a lift shaft. I had passed the 11 plus and was at Dagenham County High School. I was expected to stay on until the age of 16 and take exams, so I had to do my homework in the bus taking us to band engagements.*

I eventually specialized in bass drumming, but there was no-one available at practice sessions to teach me at first, until Elsie Spooner had the time to show me properly. Mary Turnbull, Edith's sister, taught me how to dance. As a bass drummer I wore a whole leopard skin. It was very heavy, and I sometimes had to dance in it! My memories include performing in the victory parade at

Buckingham Palace, and in a scene for the film School for Secrets *in 1946. I also played for 3 months with the Belle Vue Circus in Manchester, and did a tour of Holland. The highlight of my career with the band was the Royal Command Performance at the London Palladium in November 1947.*

One Sunday we played at a charity event at Westminster Central Hall in London. It was organized by Sylvia Pankhurst, who was very nice to us and said how much she had enjoyed the show. There was also a book fair going on that day, and she asked us each to choose a book to take away. I chose the poems of John Milton, and Miss Pankhurst wrote a dedication inside.

I'm now Chair of the Dagenham Girl Pipers Veterans' Association'.
©Ivy Richards 2010

Vicky Arnold (in the band 1944-54)

'*I was 11 when I joined the band. My sister took me to a display by the band and that inspired me very much. I was very nervous at my first band practice. Once I learned to read music, I found playing the pipes easier. My first tune apart from the exercises on the recorder was probably* Highland Laddie, *although my favourite tune was* Black Bear.

Lots of highlights stick in my mind, two in particular: 1947, appearing in a Royal Command Performance at the London Palladium; 1952-53, in a show on Broadway New York in the Latin Quarter nightclub, and also doing a police benefit concert in Madison Square Garden and meeting lots of celebrities and getting autographs (Tyrone Power and Bette Davis were my most memorable). ...Another highlight in New York was doing a show at the West Point Marine Base. We had lots of amusing incidents and it was always fun being in the band, especially as we all got on so well together. I left the band to get married in 1954.
©Vicky Arnold 2010

Kathleen Howell (in the band 1946-52)

'*I enjoyed every moment of first band practice. I didn't find the pipes difficult to learn, as I had a wonderful teacher, Hilda Creffield. The first tune I mastered was* Sean Trews. *We had to learn to read bagpipe music and learn to read about 400 pieces off by heart. We practiced on a chanter so it wasn't too noisy when we practised at home. We not only had to learn to play the bagpipes, we had also to master the side-drum, tenor drum and Highland dancing.*

Highlights of my time with the band include performing at the Chelsea Arts Ball in the Royal Albert Hall on New Year's Eve. We never knew which instrument we would be called upon to play when out on engagements. I also trained under Winnie Pile to become Drum Major. I enjoyed every minute of my time with the Band. It's how I spent my youth. It meant everything to me'.
©Kathleen Howell 2010

Doris Warren (in the band from 1951)

'*I was 12 when I joined the band. I lived at Halbutt Street and attended Halbutt Street Girls School. I joined because my friends were all members. I was quite scared at first practice, and found the pipes difficult to learn. Eventually I specialized in drumming. Memories of my time with the band include being on the Isle of Wight at the time of the Coronation. I also vividly remember touring Scotland, and meeting members of the Black Watch. I sent some of my earnings from that tour home to my Mum as a deposit for a new gas cooker. I had to leave the band after I hurt my ankle dancing'.* ©Doris Warren 2010

Alma Behn (in the band 1953-61)

'*What a wonderful experience it was, being an Essex Girl who joined the Dagenham Girl Pipers. To work at so many places whether here or abroad, they all have special memories. These include performing at the Brussels World Fair in 1958, at a Buckingham Palace garden party, at Army bases in Germany and at Princes Street Gardens in Edinburgh. One year, I won the Pipe Major's Cup for piping. My last major engagement was at the Lido in Paris (a 3 month contract that lasted 2 years) alongside the Bluebell Girls. I did go back with my husband in 1999 to visit the Lido again and see the show. It's a pity Elvis Presley wasn't in the audience then like he was in 1959!*' ©Alma Behn 2010

Hazel Arkle (in the band 1958-c1967)

'*I was 13 years old when I joined the band. I saw an article in the* Dagenham Post *about it, I thought it sounded a bit exciting and a bit different from Brownies or Girl Guides...The first time I went to the Drill Hall (which was then in Halbutt Street), the sound of the pipes made the hair on the back of my neck stand up, especially when the whole band played together.*

I wasn't really any good at the bagpipes. I was a tenor drummer, then a side drummer, and also a dancer which I loved very much. I think my first performance probably would have been an agricultural show, as we did a lot of them up and down the country in the summer, but I think my first big show was at Wembley with the Harlem Globetrotters.

As soon as I left school I was just 15, I was taken on my first trip abroad with the band to work at the Lido nightclub in Paris. I had never flown before so this was all a new experience for me...a few of the stars that came in were Adam Faith, Charlie Drake, Sophie Tucker, Yul Brynner, John Wayne, Coco Chanel, plus Frank Sinatra and Dean Martin who always caused a stir with the audience wanting autographs so Madame Bluebell took them to her office to watch the show from there. Elvis Presley also came to watch the show, but unfortunately I was at home on holiday so missed him.

As I was only 15, I had to go to the British Consulate once every month to let them know I was okay and well taken care of...Later I appeared in a circus in Barcelona for 2 or 3 months. I also took part in a South American trip to Venezuela and went on the South Africa tour for 3 months, a beautiful country.

My time in the band was a happy time and I felt proud to wear the uniform. The girls were the most fun to be with and we had a lot of laughs. I have very fond memories and consider it to be some of the happiest years of my life'.
©Hazel Arkle 2010

Sandra Yard (in the band 1958-68)

'I was 11 when I joined the band. I joined because I loved the music. – I used to hear the band practising on my way home from school. At my first band practice I was nervous but excited. The pipes were difficult to learn but with hard work and dedication they were mastered. The 'stiff finger' technique took some learning. The tunes first learnt were, I believe, Scotland the Brave *and* Highland Laddie...

My first time abroad at the age of 13 to France (Calais) was really memorable. I specialized in piping but dancing and drumming were also enjoyable.

The highlights were too numerous to mention, but here are a few: Pantomimes with Gerry Marsden (Gerry & the Pacemakers) and Mr Pastry (Richard Hearne). Blackpool Tower Circus for six months (I enjoyed meeting the lions!). Going to Glasgow and appearing for a season on the Jimmy Logan Show (imagine an all-girl English bagpipe band impressing Scottish audiences!). A TV appearance with Charlie Drake. Touring Israel, South America and South Africa. Meeting celebrities such as Roger Moore, Maurice Chevalier, Bob Hope, Bing Crosby and many, many more.

One amusing incident sticks in my mind. We were performing at the Royal Albert Hall in a V Dance formation, with me in front, positioned in the point of the V doing a Highland Fling, when my sporran fell off in mid-dance. This did bring a smile to the faces of the Royalty in the audience, but my Pipe Major of the time was not amused!

I left the band in 1968 as I had met my future husband-to-be and he was touring with his band and we wanted to travel together.

I would like to dedicate my input to my dear mum Gladys, who sadly passed away in 2007. She called herself a "Piper Mum" and loved the band and was always there for me'. ©Sandra Yard 2010

Valerie Sitch (in the band from 1949)

'*I lived at Verney Road and attended Halbutt Street School. I was 11 when I joined the band. My father was a Ford worker, and had a friend at work who had four sisters in the band. I didn't find the pipes were difficult to learn, and I remember the first tune I mastered was* Over the sea to Skye. *I specialized in dancing and drumming.*

The highlight of my time with the band was touring Australia in 1953-4. We met the Queen in Sydney. I celebrated my 16th birthday in Australia and Tommy Trinder called me out on stage that evening and announced it!
©Valerie Sitch 2010

Anita Fenn (in the band 1966-1969)

'*My sister Sharon joined the band two years before me. I couldn't wait till I turned 11 to join. We joined the band mainly for something to keep us occupied, but once joining we became dedicated, and I must admit I loved performing.*

My first performance was at Wembley Arena when the Harlem Globetrotters were playing, and we performed in the intervals. I must have had the oldest sporran going – as soon as I started to dance, the chain broke, and it was hanging down and bouncing around...I pulled it off (still dancing) and threw it behind me. Once I returned back to my drum, I had to kick the sporran out of the way, so no one tripped over it. I think I must have been about 12 at the time!

I was a side drummer, and also won the Lily Evans Dancing Cup. My father Kenneth Fenn was awarded something as well, as he used to re-paint the drums and polish the swords, so it was quite a family affair.

I have wonderful memories of my time in the band: the practice nights, the performances, and the great friendships. I am proud to tell anyone that I was a Dagenham Girl Piper, it's my claim to fame!'   ©Anita Fenn 2010

Note: the girls are referred to in this chapter by their maiden names, as this is how they were known within the band.

Tenor drummer Joyce Reeland with the band on parade through Dagenham in the 1930s *(LBBD Archives at Valence House)*

SOURCES AND FURTHER READING

The band's archive records (such as the Company Orders) are scattered and do not seem to have survived in their entirety. The main sources for this book have been newspaper articles (chiefly from the *Dagenham Post* and the *Barking Advertiser*), written memoirs, and interviews with former and current band members.

Sometimes the sources have differed and it has been difficult to confirm points of fact. If any errors have unintentionally crept in, I will be more than happy to correct them in future editions.

Original sources held at Barking & Dagenham Archives, Valence House:

Scrapbook of photographs, press cuttings and correspondence covering World War Two and the 1940s

Oral history recordings made by former band members, including Pipe Major Peggy Iris

Photographs, theatre programmes, music books and other material donated by members of the band. Valence House is always very grateful to receive donations of Dagenham Girl Pipers photographs and other memorabilia so that they can be preserved for posterity. If you can help, please e-mail localstudies@lbbd.gov.uk

Books:

Alfred HAYNES: *The Dagenham Girl Pipers* (Faber & Faber, 1957)
Mickey CHILD: *One of a kind – notes on memoirs of a Pied Piper* (privately published, 2010)

Booklets published by the Dagenham Girl Pipers:

Piping through the War (1945)
Dagenham's Piping Ambassadors (1952)
The Pipers from Dagenham (c.1955)
The Dagenham Girl Pipers (c.1957)
Tartan and Lace (c.1958)

Article in the *Daily Mail* entitled "The Reunion", 24 December 1999, pp. 30-31 (a preview of the band's Millennium Day Reunion)

ACKNOWLEDGEMENTS

I'm especially grateful to the following, who responded immediately and generously to my first tentative suggestion of a publication. This book would not exist without their help and support throughout. They are:

- **The Dagenham Girl Pipers Veterans' Association** committee: **Grace Simmonds** (Secretary), **Ivy Riley** (Chair) and **Leon Simmonds** (Treasurer). As well as offering information, photographs and general support, they kindly placed an article in the Association newsletter appealing for former band members to send me memories and photographs

- **Richard Chapman**, who very generously lent me the large collection of newspaper cuttings and images of the band built up by him and his late brother **Ken Chapman**

- **Brook Land** and **Karen Mahoney** of the **David Land Agency** (the band's management) for their great help and support, in particular by allowing the use of their wonderful photographs

Pipe Major **Peggy Iris,** Pipe Major **Sheila Hatcher** (formerly Nobes) and Sergeant **Iris Hamilton** (formerly Toleman) deserve special thanks for answering my endless questions, and for allowing me to use photographs and other material from their personal collections.

So many other band members past and present have also been unfailingly helpful, particularly (in alphabetical order): **Hazel Arkle** (now Gunn); **Vicky Arnold** (now Nicholls); **Alma Behn** (now King); **Margaret Child** (now Cullum); **Janet Coster** (now Stevens); **Shirley Duffin** (now Lovick); **Anita Fenn**; **Lily Field**; **Kathleen Howell** (now Batten);**Valerie Sitch** (now Elder); **Jean Vale** (now Gibbins); **Lily Vale** (now Williamson); **Doris Warren** (now Taylor); **Linda Webb** (now Lilburne); **Jan Wells** (now Goodyear); **Bette White** (now Read); **Pat Whitworth** (now Ryder); and **Sandra Yard** (now Jones).

I am also grateful to **Tony Clifford; Vic Pountney; Clive Simpson; Iain Cameron; Frank Baron; Paul Bennett** of the *Barking & Dagenham Post;* **Danny Howell** of the *Daily Mail* for permission to use quotes from its Millennium reunion article; and **Hayley Charlton** for the cover design.

Thanks are also due to my colleagues at Valence House Museum for their support, particularly **John Porter** and **Tahlia Coombs** for assistance with photographs, and **Mark Watson** for his Photoshopping skills on the front cover image.

If anyone has been inadvertently omitted, I will be happy to correct this in future editions.

Lightning Source UK Ltd.
Milton Keynes UK
UKHW05f2042080718
325397UK00003B/47/P